WELL DONE

DISCOVERING GOD'S GRACE AND DEMAND IN DISCIPLESHIP

RICHARD E. MENNINGER

Well Done: Discovering God's Grace and Demand in Discipleship

ISBN: 979-8-9852118-0-1 (paperback), 979-8-9852118-1-8 (epub)

Editor: Beth Lottig
Publishing and Design Services: MelindaMartin.me

To my beloved wife, Gaynia,
whose love made me a better man.

Contents

Acknowledgments

Although writing a book requires countless hours of solitary work, it soon becomes apparent that in order to produce the finished project, the help and support of many is needed. The words I offer here can only begin to express the heartfelt gratitude I have for those who aided in this journey.

I am grateful to God for providing me the opportunity to write this book. Along the way He granted me health, insight, perseverance, and, most importantly, persons who gave me strength and encouragement to keep going.

I want to acknowledge my appreciation for the students—especially Christian Study majors—of Ottawa University who allowed me the privilege to "think out loud." Their affirmation, questions, challenges, and insights proved invaluable in providing me the motivation and opportunity to identify "what I believe and why I believe it."

I want to thank Angie Zachary of Affordable Christian Editing for editing my work and for referring me to Beth Lottig of Inspire Books. Beth provided assurance and expertise in helping me navigate the potentially treacherous waters of self-publishing. In turn, she referred me to

Melinda Martin of Martin Publishing Services, whose skill and transparency relieved much of the stress associated with the publishing of this book.

I can only begin to relate how important my family has been. My wife, Gaynia, has continually supported my journey in theological studies and has always shown confidence in me, even when I had no confidence. She, along with my family, encouraged me to write this book, all the while showing patience as I attempted to gain traction in the new world of retirement.

Finally, it is my prayer that through this book readers will discover the grace of God to a greater degree. If this be the case, then all I can say is *soli Deo gloria.*

ONE

INTRODUCTION

Most of us are undoubtedly familiar with the story of Captain Chesley Sullenberger III, "Sully," who safely landed a jet airliner without engine power on the Hudson River in New York in January of 2009. He had two to three minutes to decide what to do when the engines shut down because the aircraft flew through a flock of Canadian geese. He reacted correctly, and all on board were rescued without injury. Sullenberger was not born with the ability to fly—let alone land a crippled plane on water. He transformed his interest in flying into a commitment to be the best pilot he could be. His dedication drove him to undertake the training needed to become a pilot. The endless repetition of assignments, the constant effort and concentration to perform seemingly mundane tasks, prepared Captain Sullenberger for this dramatic day on the cold Hudson.

While the "miracle on the Hudson" is an extraordinary accomplishment, I come away with a nagging question: Was the captain a great pilot before this event or only afterward? That is, how many other pilots as qualified as

Captain Sullenberger never receive such widespread acclaim for their service and skill, in spite of a career of dedicated work and a spotless safety record? Is the difference a matter of talent or opportunity? When all is said and done, is it only Sullenberger who should be judged as having performed a job "well done," or is such praise fitting for other pilots as well?

In similar fashion, the vast majority of Christians face the vexing issue of whether their work for Christ will receive the blessed commendation from His lips of, "Well done, good and faithful servant." This concern is particularly pressing. It is easy to second guess our importance, especially when there is little indication that our service to God makes a lasting difference. As a result, we are prone to ask ourselves whether we have failed to produce despite what God has invested in us. We wonder why we weren't given the talent to make a difference, even in service to the local church.

This struggle is made worse when "talented" Christians tell those struggling with these concerns that they are as important as those who stand out. The use of this familiar cliché can come across as patronizing. In this book, I present the case for seeing that all we do for Christ is important, provided it is done to glorify God. The words "well done" will greet those who have proven trustworthy in following Christ, who are faithful stewards of God's resources, even though their effort for Christ is unknown to most. Discipleship worthy of Christ is about faithfully discharging our duties; it is the challenge to be the best we can be with the riches we have been given.

To follow Jesus in genuine discipleship is to accept *both* God's grace and His demand. The latter is not a heavy-handed mandate that God places on us as an ultimatum to meet an impossible standard. Rather, it is an invitation to "glorify God and enjoy him forever."[1] If we want to relish our walk with God, we cannot do so unless we recognize He must grant us the tools, as well as the desire and strength, to live our discipleship to the fullest. It is a sobering truth of Scripture that our salvation is to be demonstrated in our discipleship, for to call ourselves Christians yet live as though we have not experienced the grace of God is a serious indictment. This suggests that we have fallen prey to the popular notion that we can be believers in Christ without being followers. If this is so, we are headed for either a life that does little to honor God or, worse, one which does not possess the salvation we think is ours.

The *purpose* of this book is to show that the words "well done" are reserved for all dedicated disciples of our Lord and not just for those few who always seem to reside in the spotlight. God does not give the same resources to His people, and this is as it should be. God uses us where we can flourish in Him, in ways that are unique. No template can be placed on our Christian lives that will have a "one-size-fits-all" outcome. Yet all disciples are called to fulfill the demand of God's grace. For Jesus to pronounce that a life

1 Question One, *Westminster Shorter Catechism.*

lived for Him is deserving of a "well done" is to acknowledge a life of faithfulness as judged by our Lord.

The Call to Discipleship

When Jesus called His disciples in the Gospels, He was offering "the blessings of salvation," including discipleship.[2] His call to "follow Me" is a summons directed to us with the expectation that we will seek to live "with a total commitment and in an exclusive relationship to one who is recognized as not just a teacher but the Messiah" (Matthew 4:18–22).[3] God calls us into His kingdom (1 Thessalonians 2:12) through Christ (Philippians 3:19) and His gospel (2 Thessalonians 2:14) into fellowship with Jesus Christ our Lord (1 Corinthians 1:9).

When we speak of the *call* in biblical terms, it almost exclusively refers to our following Christ and not to following a vocation or career path.[4] That is, according to Scripture, our call is simply to trust in Him for salvation and to live as His disciples everywhere and with everyone. But such an understanding becomes a challenge, for many in society feel "called" to perform a certain occupation, without any reference to or awareness of the idea of the biblical call. Even

---

2 K. Schmidt, *kaleō*, in Geoffrey Bromiley *Theological Dictionary of the New Testament Abridged Volume* (Grand Rapids, MI: Eerdmans, 1985), 394–395.

3 G. Kittel, *akoloutheō*, in Bromiley, *Theological Dictionary*, 33.

4 Marco Rotman, "Vocation in Theology and Psychology: Conflicting Approaches?" *Christian Higher Education*, 2017, Vol. 16, Nos. 1–2, 23–32.

Christians can use the term to mean different things in different contexts. That is, we can confess Jesus as Lord and acknowledge we have heard His call to follow Him, and in the same breath say we are sensing a call to marry someone or pursue a particular career.

We need to recognize that we have a *primary calling* (that is the call to follow Christ), which is to be lived out through several *secondary callings*, such as our home, church, community, and vocation.[5] In other words, our principal calling is to live as Christ's disciples, seeking to have "lip and life" point to what God has done in the cross and the empty tomb, offering hope and peace to a struggling world. We must be reminded that we should be His disciples in our homes, churches, communities, and vocations where He has placed us. Discipleship is initiated in responding to the primary call, and we demonstrate we take this call seriously by being His disciples in our secondary callings. The correct understanding of call need not be confusing as long as we understand Christ calls us to Himself and sends us out to be His people in our daily lives:

> This vital distinction between primary and secondary calling carries with it two challenges—first to hold the two together and, second, to ensure that they are kept in the right order. In other words, if we understand calling, we

5 Gene Edward Veith Jr., *God at Work: Your Christian Vocation in All of Life* (Wheaton, IL: Crossway, 2002), 47.

> must make sure that first things remain first and the primary calling always comes before the secondary calling. But we must also make sure that our primary calling leads without fail to the secondary calling.[6]

Christianity has not helped matters when educating the church and the world regarding the truth behind calling. Far too often the concept of a call in Christian circles is focused on either entering the ministry or discovering a satisfying career. To speak of full-time Christian ministry or our secular careers and jobs as our call tends to limit our view of discipleship and leaves us open to frustration and doubt as to our usefulness to God. When Jesus calls us to discipleship, we all receive the same call.

A *disciple* is one who responds to the call of Christ to accept Him as Savior and follow Him in commitment and obedience. *Discipleship* is striving to speak and act in this world as Jesus would. Our goal should be to allow God to use us to redeem every moment, every situation for Him, including the times when active service is called for, encouragement is needed, or resistance to the world's way of thinking is the only way to honor Christ. The disciple who is truly of the Lord will be on alert 24/7:

> Mostly God asks us to be faithful in little things—especially relationships. Small expressions of negativity can quickly add up and

6 Os Guinness. *The Call: Finding and Fulfilling the Central Purpose of Your Life* (Nashville: W Publishing Group, 2003), 31.

> disrupt our relationships without us even realizing it. It takes vigilance in the small things to fulfill God's plan for us: to be the look on His face, the tone of His voice, and the touch of His hand. You are to represent His presence and His love. You are placed where you are to make His mercy and faithfulness visible and concrete.[7]

This is the disciple whom Christ praises. Our Lord knows our heart and the resources given to us to live for Him. He is aware if we have given our all, no matter how the world or even other Christians judge us. The playing field is level, for all disciples are judged on how they fulfill the call of God. Where we differ is, we will live out this primary call in what can be identified as our particular secondary callings, specific to our family, our community, our local church, and, most visibly, our vocation. Since each of these callings find followers of Christ in unique situations, we can easily misjudge one way or the other whether certain Christians are worthy disciples because we base our determination on worldly standards. But to do so is to misunderstand what characterizes genuine discipleship as sought by Christ when He calls us. We all hear and respond to the same call, and we all live out this call through the secondary callings, which are unique to our circumstances.

---

7 Paul D. Tripp, *New Morning Mercies* (Wheaton: Crossway, 2014), reading for November 10.

The words of Jesus, "Follow Me," are by far the most important words we will ever have directed at us. The reality behind this invitation will change our future forever! It is the only summons that will provide life (1 John 5:20) and grant us true freedom (John 8:32). This is the grace of discipleship. But, follower, beware! "Whoever does not carry their cross and follow me cannot be my disciple" (Luke14:27). This informs us that:

> Such grace is *costly* because it calls us to follow, and it is grace because it calls us to follow *Jesus Christ*. It is costly because it costs a man His life, and it is grace because it gives a man the only true life. It is costly because it condemns sin and grace because it justifies the sinner. Above all, it is *costly* because it cost God the life of His Son: "ye were bought at a price," and what has cost God much cannot be cheap for us. Above all, it is *grace* because God did not reckon His Son too dear a price to pay for our life but delivered Him up for us. Costly grace is the Incarnation of God.[8]

We must avoid cheap grace, which "is grace without discipleship, grace without the cross, grace without Jesus Christ, living and incarnate."[9] The grace and demand of discipleship

---

8 Dietrich Bonhoeffer, *The Cost of Discipleship* (New York: Touchstone, 1995), 45.

9 Bonhoeffer, *The Cost of Discipleship*, 45.

is captured in its essence in Dietrich Bonhoeffer's famous quote, "When Christ calls a man, He bids him come and die."[10]

Grace Is a Many Splendored Thing

Grace is simply the loving actions God showered on creation, especially the elect: "See what great love the Father has lavished on us, that we should be called children of God! And that is what we are!" (1 John 3:1). The concept of grace comes easily to those who have accepted Christ as their Savior. It is not uncommon for Christians to recite Ephesians 2:8–9: "For it is by grace you have been saved, through faith—and this is not from yourselves, it is the gift of God—not by works, so that no one can boast." In addition, the words of the first verse of the beloved hymn "Amazing Grace" reinforce the idea that a loving and merciful God has graciously rescued us from eternal punishment. And this is definitely so! But unfortunately, it seems that our understanding of grace often goes no further, for many fail to perceive that grace is all-consuming and intended to saturate our entire lives, now and forevermore.

Jerry Bridges opens his book *Transforming Grace* with this observation: "The grace of God is one of the most important subjects in all of Scripture. At the same time, it is probably one of the least understood."[11] The apostle Paul would undoubtedly agree, especially when examining

---

10 Bonhoeffer, *The Cost of Discipleship*, 89.

11 Jerry Bridges, *Transforming Grace: Living Confidently in God's Unfailing Love* (Colorado Springs, CO: Navpress, 1991), 11.

the connection between discipleship and grace. He uses his opening words in 1 Corinthians 15 to set the stage for one of the richest verses in the New Testament: "But by the grace of God I am what I am, and his grace to me was not without effect. No, I worked harder than all of them—yet not I, but the grace of God that was with me" (15:10).

After reminding his readers they have received the saving message of the gospel (15:2), Paul shares that Christ appeared to him as to the other apostles and, even though he persecuted the church, God's grace nevertheless rescued him and put him on the true path (15:8–9). Paul is telling us that grace reached out to him, resulting in his salvation, transformation, and life of discipleship, especially in ministering to the Gentiles. If Paul were here today, he would simply share that "God saves those whom he calls; it is all God and all grace. He saved me, and He changed me. Furthermore, He gave me a ministry like no other. It was through my destiny to be a 'light to the Gentiles' that He made me who I am." He teaches us that the investment God makes in us at our salvation (Romans 8:32) is to be returned to Him in and through our faithful discipleship.

In order to appreciate both the depth and richness of God's grace as revealed in our discipleship, we must first comprehend that the foundation of our life in Christ is simply the fact of grace: "We believe it is through the grace of our Lord Jesus that we are saved" (Acts 15:11, ESV). This is not simply an event of the past, for Jesus' death on the cross is the "power of God" which saves us (1 Corinthians 1:18, present tense). Moreover, Romans 5:8 tells us that "God demonstrates his love" in the cross, for "it is an event of the past, but it keeps showing the love of God in the present."[12] In highlighting the cross as a means for experiencing the grace of God, we uphold Scripture. However, we must present a balanced picture of grace, for we can easily minimize the importance of the resurrection and its relevance to discipleship.

The resurrection can be viewed merely as an "epilogue to the great story of Jesus' sacrifice on the cross . . . This is unfortunate, because a cross without a resurrection is a cross stripped of power, devoid of meaning, and unable to save."[13] With the resurrection of Christ, we have proof that God's kingdom has invaded this sinful world; and we have new life, now and forevermore. We must not fail to appreciate that the grace offered at salvation is a gift that keeps on giving. The new life we are given is to become the basis for living in God's presence for eternity.

This concept of the "totality of salvation" (1 Corinthians 15:2) refers to an ongoing process which is overlooked when grace (*charis*) is simply defined as salvation from hell, a result of unmerited favor. While grace is definitely something we do not deserve, we tend to make it linear or one-dimensional. Rather, grace is "three-dimensional," much more robust and life-changing than simply salvation from God's wrath.

---

12 Leon Morris, *The Epistle to the Romans* (Grand Rapids, MI: Eerdmans, 1998), 224 n. 27.

13 Casey Lute, *"But God . . . ": The Two Words at the Heart of the Gospel* (Adelphi, MD: CruciformPress, 2011), 64–65.

It also includes our growth in holiness and our opportunities to serve God: His call is to come to Him for salvation and follow His Son in discipleship. And embedded in discipleship are our opportunities to live for Him as we fulfill our callings. When we understand His call to us in light of His grace, we see that grace is His unconditional love for us as demonstrated in our salvation, transformation, and participation in healing His creation.

If we are to equip ourselves to understand how discipleship works in our lives, we must accept and flourish in the truth that our lives are to be lived in light of the cross and the empty tomb. Without Christ taking our penalty and paying the debt for our sin, we have no access to God; without the bodily resurrection, we have no power or hope to be used of God and to be "a chosen people, a royal priesthood, a holy nation, God's special possession" (1 Peter 2:9). Our discipleship is to be grace-filled and grace-driven. Becoming a disciple is an act of grace, but it does not stop with our salvation; rather, "the entire living of the Christian life can be seen to result from the continuous bestowal of grace."[14]

The Grammar of Grace

When God's grace meets us and we first experience His mercy, we are granted the privilege of living in the new creation (2 Corinthians 5:17). Furthermore, "Our citizenship is in heaven" (Philippians 3:20), for we are "foreigners and strang-

---

14 Wayne Grudem, *Systematic Theology: An Introduction to Biblical Doctrine* (Grand Rapids: Zondervan, 1994), 201.

ers on earth" (Hebrews 11:13), even aliens (1 Peter 2:11). A new situation confronts us, for life now "is a tale of two cities . . . an inescapable tension!"[15] We discover living out our faith in Christ is a struggle, for spiritual forces oppose us (Ephesians 6:10–18); and we are engaged in a constant battle against the world (1 John 2:15–17).

Theologians have captured the essence of this war by employing simple grammatical terms. They use the indicative and imperative moods to show the constant tension between who we are and how we are to live. The *indicative* is simply a statement of fact, and the *imperative* is a command. In theological terms, God has acted (indicative) to make us His people; yet we are commanded (imperative) to live like His people because often we do not. For example, Paul writes that we can find freedom from the tyranny of sin, "for we know that our old self was crucified with him so that the body ruled by sin might be done away with, that we should no longer be slaves to sin—because anyone who has died has been set free from sin" (Romans 6:6–7). Yet this reference to the indicative is soon followed by the imperative: "Therefore do not let sin reign in your mortal body so that you obey its evil desires" (6:12). The correct way to interpret the grace and demand of discipleship is to follow this line of thinking: You must *become who you are.*

---

15 Ian Hamilton, "Living in Two Worlds," April 13, 2012, accessed February 3, 2021, <https://banneroftruth.org/us/resources/articles/2012/living-in-twoworlds/>.

The mercies of God have been realized (indicative); based on this action, Paul commands the Romans to be transformed (imperative). This description reflects the joining of grace and demand in pursuing discipleship. Since God has acted to redeem us through His Son's death, does not such love have the right to expect that we should live like His Son?

We should note that the indicative requires the imperative since we are sinful, but that the latter can be realized only because of the former. The potential to live like Christ is within our grasp because of God's grace, for He has provided us with "everything we need for life and godliness" to live a life worthy of our name, a child of God (2 Peter 1:3–11). We do not have the right to ignore the need to live as God demands. But no matter the difficulties in living for Christ, the call to follow Him in discipleship is a privilege and the only way to fulfillment and purpose. To follow Jesus is both grace and demand from our Lord: "Those who have been grasped by the indicative must also be grasped by the imperative."[16]

Dedicated discipleship can only be understood correctly in light of God's grace, in what He has given us (chapter two), what He has done for us (chapter three), and what He demands of us (chapters four and five). I will explore how grace is the basis for what we can do for God, including our particular spheres of influence, whether it is in our home,

---

16 Thomas R. Schreiner, *Paul Apostle of God's Glory in Christ: A Pauline Theology* (Downers Grove: InterVarsity Press, 2001), 260.

our church, our community, or our place of work (chapters six through nine). Those who call Jesus Savior and Lord do not have the option of living for Christ. Our discipleship is to be shaped by the thought that we are salt and light and are commanded to be Christ's ambassadors in our unique way, living obediently to what the Bible teaches and avoiding the pitfalls and temptations of our flesh. Discipleship is as much about who we are as what we do, regardless of how many people see our work or appreciate what we do. The life of discipleship is graciously given to us with great expectation in return.

TWO

Talent Show

It is told that pastor and philanthropist John Fredrick Oberlin (1740–1826) found himself in a terrible snowstorm once when crossing the Alps. He was rescued and taken to safety by another traveler. The rescuer would not reveal his name. Frustrated, an argument ensued because Oberlin wanted to reward the one who rescued him, or at least pray for him by name. The one who came to the aid of Oberlin finally asked, "Do you know the name of the good Samaritan in the parable?" "No," said Oberlin, "scripture does not tell us that." "Well," said the rescuer, "there is no need to know mine."[17] The unnamed rescuer wanted no recognition, though no doubt he derived satisfaction that his Lord knew of his deeds (Matthew 25:31–46). An important reason behind this book is that many Christians serve Christ in relative anonymity.

The foundational passage for our study is Matthew 25:14–30, and correctly interpreting these verses is crucial for com-

---

17 William Barclay, *And Jesus Said: A Handbook on the Parables of Jesus* (Philadelphia, PA: Westminster Press, 1970), 109.

prehending the full meaning of discipleship. Of the four Gospels, Matthew stands out as the most influential in the early centuries of Christianity, mainly due to its usefulness as a manual on discipleship. It is no accident that Matthew introduces the demand of discipleship early in his Gospel when Jesus tells the disciples, "You are the salt of the earth . . . You are the light of the world" (Matthew 5:13, 14); he then concludes Jesus' public ministry with the statement that faithful discipleship will be recognized by the glorious words, "Well done, good and faithful servant!" (25:21). Essentially, then, these two thoughts open and close Matthew's teaching concerning following Jesus as Lord.

Our passage under study is a parable, part of a series of parables found in Jesus' discussion of the end times in Matthew 24–25. These two chapters together number approximately one hundred verses, yet, significantly, almost two-thirds is not a description of how the world ends but insight on how to be prepared when it happens. Such urgency applies to our lives whether we point to the second coming or to our death. Uncertainty concerning the time of Christ's return becomes a non-issue; rather, the certainty of His return is what matters and what drives our work for Him in this life.[18]

The storyline of the parable is the common practice of a wealthy person entrusting his possessions to his servants

---

18 Donald A. Hagner, *Matthew 14–28* (Dallas, TX: Word Books, 1995), 716.

in order to earn more profits. To the first servant the master gives five talents, to the second two talents, and to the third one talent, "each according to his ability" (25:15).[19] While their master is away on a journey, the first two servants proceed to double their respective allotments, but the third servant buries his. When the master returns, he settles the accounts with his servants.

The first two servants produce their returns on the master's investment. As a result, both *receive the same commendation*: "Well done, good and faithful servant! You have been faithful with a few things; I will put you in charge of many things. Come and share your master's happiness!" (25:21). However, the third servant is condemned for not producing a return on his one talent, to the extent that the master calls him wicked, lazy, and worthless and his talent is taken from him and given to the servant who now has ten. In the end, the worthless servant is banished to darkness, Matthew's description of eternal punishment (8:12; 22:13; 24:51).

When Talent Isn't Enough

This parable is probably familiar to many but has often been interpreted in a limited manner. This passage has been titled, "The Parable of the Talents," and herein lies a major

19 That is, "We have different gifts, according to the grace given us" (Romans 12:6). The topic of what God gives us is—as we shall see—a crucial subject.

problem with understanding the parable. The Greek term *talanton* (translated talent) is actually a sum of money and is not primarily speaking of the servants' personal abilities and skills, those naturally endowed and intended for a specific vocation or task. Our interpretation of this parable must not be influenced by the common understanding of the term *talent.*

An examination of God's grace shows that He provides salvation, sanctification, and spheres of influence, which represent the specific opportunities and responsibilities allocated to us.[20] That is, we all have different levels of influence, depending on what God has assigned to us. We don't have greater amounts of skills; we have different opportunities that are often incorrectly translated as "raw talent." I understand the use of *talent* in the parable as referring primarily to the responsibilities and opportunities a disciple has, supplemented by the skills God gives us according to who we are and what we need to do for Him on earth. While Christians possess certain skills and abilities comparable to those of other Christians, living out the primary calling in our particular secondary callings is where we differ in the number of talents given to us. Opportunities will differ in quantity and nature for each disciple. The responsibilities of ministering to those in our daily lives are the talents invested in us, even those "behind the scenes" moments in which we are involved. Our opportunities consist not

---

20 R. T. France, *Matthew, Tyndale New Testament Commentaries* (Grand Rapids: Eerdmans, 1985), 352.

only of sharing the gifts God places in our hands to help others but also standing firm in the face of opposition. This is the full spectrum of discipleship. This parable is teaching that those who are in a Lord-servant relationship with Jesus Christ have been entrusted with a portfolio that equips and qualifies them to serve God throughout their lives and—if conscientiously pursued—places them in the position to be praised by Christ for their efforts.

If the idea of talent is restricted only to skills and abilities from God, such an interpretation implies that those with fewer talents are less valuable. The servant with five talents is more appreciated by his master because his return is greater than the servant with two. Furthermore, if we are not recognized as having great talent, then our work for Christ is downplayed. Those who are visible and applauded for their service are seen as more talented and blessed than those whose work for Christ often goes unnoticed. We can easily miss the overall theme of this parable: Those who follow Christ have been equipped to fulfill the privilege and duty to live as His disciples in a way that honors the Father and points the way to Him. The "talents" given to us who believe in Christ as Savior and Lord pave the way for faithful discipleship and fulfillment as we become all that we are meant to be.

In God's eyes each servant was equally important and useful to God (Luke 19:11–13). The more talented servant didn't have a greater amount of skill; he simply had different opportunities. This is an indictment of the way we assess work for God. The greater the acclaim, the more the publicity, the grander the awards; this is how we judge talented disciples. But to do so is to misunderstand this parable and, in turn, misconstrue what discipleship is all about. We are to faithfully carry out our responsibilities, no matter whether they are great or small. The master allocates talents as He places us where He wants us to bring Him glory. Not everyone can lead a large ministry or organization; not everyone can faithfully shepherd a shut-in program in the community. We are called to faithfully fulfill the talents entrusted to us.

A closer look at this parable offers more insight. The first two servants demonstrated they loved their master and proved it by faithfulness in providing a return on his investment. Their relationship to their master was not established by their work, but rather it was demonstrated by their service to him. Jesus' disciples did not earn salvation by works (Ephesians 2:8–9), but their productive discipleship "is evidence as to whether he or she is truly one of Jesus' own."[21] Living a life that shows Jesus is Lord is not an option; those of us who call on His name are to be different in what we do, why we do it, and who we are. Jesus' disciples—then and now—must live transformed lives (another example of the grace of God). Such lives demonstrate our love of God by seeking "first his kingdom and his righteousness" in all we do (Matthew 6:33). The disciple receiving the praise of

---

21 Michael J. Wilkins, *Matthew, The NIV Application Commentary* (Grand Rapids, MI: Zondervan, 2004), 808.

Christ ("well done") is the one who faithfully utilized God's investment to contribute to the work of His kingdom.

Our conscientious stewardship of what God gives us to live while on the earth is summed up in the concept of faithful discipleship. The lack of the same was the undoing of the third servant: to not live as the "salt and the light" revealed he was a servant in name only. Had the third servant produced a one-talent return, he would have received the same commendation as the other two.

Though all three servants were given their respective amount of responsibility based on the sovereign purpose of God, we note that the first two received identical praise though the amount of their endowments differed. The different amounts were not based on God loving the first servant more or determining that the second was not essential to Him and His work; rather, the differing amounts were based on responsibilities. Each disciple of Christ is given spiritual resources, as well as responsibilities, opportunities, and tasks to perform that differ from person to person. Some resources are for many to see, and some are in the background, hidden from sight. A *hierarchy of visibility* figures into play when certain responsibilities are carried out. The truth is that some actions are more visible—though not more valuable—than others, and it is here that we may find Christians struggling with identity and self-esteem when they compare themselves and their witness to that of those around them. And matters are only made worse when those with "less" talent are told by those with "more" talent that their work is still as important. Such talk conveys a condescending attitude, an unintended consequence of failing to understand correctly what Jesus meant by the master's property in Matthew 25:14. This becomes demoralizing when focusing specifically on spiritual achievements and responsibilities in the church.

To make matters worse, Christians can develop a skewed approach to serving God. Hugh Whelchel, executive director of the Institute for Faith, Work & Economics, struggled with integrating his Christian faith with his professional life. He confesses:

> Vocationally, I was working in the business world. If you had asked me then to describe the work I was doing that was important to God, I would have told you about my work in the lay leadership of my church, the adult Sunday school class that I taught, and the work I did with Christian non-profit groups. I secretly envied pastors, missionaries, and others who got to work 'full-time' for God. I saw little if no connection between what I did as a businessman and God's kingdom.[22]

Thankfully, he came to understand that "my vocational work was part of a larger grand story of God."[23] When

22 Hugh Whelchel, *How Then Should We Work? Rediscovering the Biblical Doctrine of Work* (Bloomington, IN: WestBow Press, 2012), xxii.

23 Whelchel, *How Then Should We Work?*, xxiii.

we apply Whelchel's thoughts about the workplace to the home, the local church, and community, we are able to grasp the idea of discipleship impacting our whole life.

On the surface, our parable can be used to support that God has intentionally supplied more gifts to some Christians than to others, and those with the lesser amounts are not as valued or useful to God's work. But such an interpretation implies a two-tiered understanding of discipleship (not unlike the first fifteen centuries of church history). One tier consists of those who are especially gifted to serve God, while the second consists of those who have "less" to contribute and "appear" less dedicated or committed. Such a picture is not what the Bible teaches.

We all stand at the foot of the cross and receive everything we have—including our abilities, opportunities, responsibilities, and unique ways of fulfilling them. God assigns different spiritual gifts and opportunities for serving the church (1 Corinthians 12:4–6). We are to fulfill our primary calling with what God has given us. Disciples who will be blessed by Jesus' words in Matthew 25:21 are the ones who took what God gave them and provided maximum return on His investment. Note that the first two servants reached their potential, for they provided a 100 percent yield on God's investment.

The two faithful servants were successful, not in worldly terms but in biblical terms, for their success resulted from using diligently—in the here and now—all that God had given them ("talents") to produce the return demanded by the master.[24] The servant with two talents' worth of the master's property was destined for smaller venues than the one with five. Whether five talents of money, or two or simply one, all amounts of investment are needed, and all servants were called to work to their fullest. While the servant with the five talents could influence more people, he may not be as much of a factor in the lives of those who needed more one-to-one input. That emphasis is reserved for the one with lesser amounts of his master's goods but with more opportunity and access to those who would never directly experience those servants with five talents. However, the latter will be able to cast his net over a wider area than one with fewer talents. Yet both spheres of influence are important to the master. In the eyes of God, there are not greater amounts of talent in terms of importance; there are simply people whose work is more widespread than others. I understand the different levels of investment (five, two, one) are from our perspective, not God's. The "talents" in the parable represent the responsibilities and skills God gives us in order to be faithful disciples, and the sooner we find our identity and contentment in what we are to do, the greater our work for God will be.

Perhaps an example will help. Many of us have watched the postgame interviews of Super Bowls. More times than not, the conversations will focus on the winning quarter-

24 Hugh Whelchel, "The Biblical Meaning of Success," Feb 9, 2014, accessed November 12, 2020, <https://www.thegospelcoalition.org/article/the-biblical-meaningof-success/>.

back. While he may offer congratulations to his offensive linemen, they will not win the most valuable player of the game award; he will. Few if any youth want to grow up and be a left tackle; no, they want to be the winning quarterback. But the head coach knows who did or did not do their job. And while his praise of those other than the quarterback will probably fall on deaf ears, he knows what makes the team successful and places it in the best position to win. The quarterback cannot be great if the linemen are not; and the linemen will not be considered successful unless the quarterback leads the team to victory. This is all in the context that the quarterback is going to receive much more in terms of responsibility (and salary!) than the linemen. But all players are equally valuable to the coach, and he clearly sees how each one is of vital importance!

What I am saying is that we must be diligent in our treatment of the Parable of the Talents, or else we fall into the trap of evaluating the effectiveness of one's discipleship (including our own) based on worldly standards. Metrics such as prestige, influence, accolades, recognition, and meeting numerical criterion (*e.g.,* souls saved, those we are discipling, etc.) can easily distort our understanding of success, whether in terms of a full-time Christian ministry or Christians making their way in the everyday world. In other words, our Lord knows His people will naturally associate other Christians with greater talent if they are receiving greater acknowledgment for their accomplishments. But we miss an important teaching when we quickly interpret this parable in such a manner. Our discipleship is not limited to "church" activities; in fact, most of it is lived out in our homes and workplaces. Paul makes it clear that we must function where we find ourselves:

> For by the grace given me I say to every one of you: Do not think of yourself more highly than you ought, but rather think of yourself with sober judgment, in accordance with the faith God has distributed to each of you. For just as each of us has one body with many members, and these members do not all have the same function, so in Christ we, though many, form one body, and each member belongs to all the others. We have different gifts, according to the grace given to each of us. If your gift is prophesying, then prophesy in accordance with your faith; if it is serving, then serve; if it is teaching, then teach; if it is to encourage, then give encouragement; if it is giving, then give generously; if it is to lead, do it diligently; if it is to show mercy, do it cheerfully. (Romans 12:3–8)

Although the apostle is referring to spiritual gifts as they relate to our work with other Christians, the principle applies to our discipleship in the home, community, and office. Our primary calling is lived out for God in our secondary callings, and we are to mark the words above.

We should not allow pride to make too much of our actions if we find ourselves in the limelight; likewise, we should not be jealous of those who are, all the while denigrating what little we have to offer. Was Paul's protégé Timothy less "talented" than Paul? Or was he simply assigned to a different sphere of influence, at least from our perspective? Was the young boy who provided the bread and the fish for the feeding of the 5,000 unimportant because we do not even know his name? (John 6:1–15). What of the one who rescued Oberlin? Are the airline pilots who didn't land a plane on the Hudson River less important than Captain Chesley Sullenberger? Are those of limited celebrity status and visibility relegated to second rank in God's kingdom? Are those providing caregiving or those overwhelmed with single parenting any less useful to God than those who speak at conferences and publish books? Will only the famous hear, "Well done"? We all serve our Lord and thus are equal whether we place the main entrée before Him or simply bus the table. The great equalizer for faithful disciples is His pronouncement of "well done," for "their achievement has been proportionately the same, however different their original endowments."[25]

As we continue our study, we do justice to this parable only when we remember that as Christians, we share the same purpose of glorifying God with our lives. We must never forget that though we serve God for the same reason, we differ in personalities, passions, respon-

25 France, *Matthew*, 354.

sibilities, and opportunities. We have different tasks that complement each other as we fulfill our purpose on earth (1 Corinthians 3:5–9).

It Is Not Who You Know

We cannot end this chapter without an important observation concerning the third servant. We must note that the two productive servants were not invited into eternal bliss because of their work, but because their output validated their relationship with their master. In this light, the third servant's lack of action is presented as sufficient evidence to assign him to eternal damnation, but not because lack of works disqualifies him from salvation. His lack of productivity demonstrates that he did not have a genuine relationship with his master.

The Parable of the Bridesmaids, which precedes the Parable of the Talents, illuminates this point (Matthew 25:1–13). The story centers around ten bridesmaids waiting to escort a wedding party to the groom's house, where the wedding feast was to take place. The parable divides the bridesmaids into five wise and five foolish ones, with the difference being the wise ones brought along oil for a possible late-night journey, and the foolish did not. As was often the case, the groom was delayed, in this instance until midnight, requiring the bridesmaids to trim their lamps. On the surface, all ten appeared prepared to attend the feast and no doubt expected to do so. However, the late-night appearance of the groom forced the unwise bridesmaids to go in search of oil instead of being in the wedding party when it entered the groom's house; the groom shut the door and when the foolish ones arrived, they were shut out. Why? Because the groom uttered what may be the most terrifying words in the Bible: "I tell you the truth, I don't know you" (25:12).

This thought of God knowing us is not always emphasized in Scripture, though it is part of the biblical picture of our relationship to God. Paul reminded the Galatians that though they know God, it is even better to "be known by God" (Galatians 4:9). This thought is crucial, for to be known by God is to be chosen by Him.[26] As J. I. Packer remarks:

> What matters supremely, therefore, is not, in the last analysis, the fact that I know God, but the larger fact which underlies it—the fact that *he knows me.* I am graven on the palms of his hands. I am never out of his mind. All my knowledge of him depends on his sustained initiative in knowing me. I know him because he first knew me and continues to know me. He knows me as a friend, one who loves me; and there is no moment when his eye is off me, or his attention distracted from me, and no moment, therefore, when his care falters.[27]

---

26 Brian S. Rosner, *Known by God: A Biblical Theology of Personal Identity* (Grand Rapids, MI: Zondervan, 2017), 96.

27 J. I. Packer, *Knowing God* (Downers Grove, IL: InterVarsity Press, 1973), 41–42.

These words describe the perspective of the master in the Parable of the Talents when he thinks of his praiseworthy servants.

Matthew elsewhere addresses the concept of being known by God. This is when Jesus declares that "religious works" do not ensure one is a Christian, a truth made painfully clear in Matthew 7:21–23:

> Not everyone who says to Me, 'Lord, Lord,' will enter the kingdom of heaven, but only he who does the will of My Father in heaven. Many will say to Me on that day, 'Lord, Lord, did we not prophesy in Your name, and in Your name drive out demons and perform many miracles?' Then I will tell them plainly, 'I never knew you; depart from Me, you evildoers!'

Here we find that many who call Jesus "Lord, Lord," and even prophesy and perform miracles and exorcisms in His name, will hear words similar to what the foolish bridesmaids heard: "I don't know you." One could easily think such people were at least "five-talent" disciples if not more. But they fail to do the will of God, which is to follow Christ in motive as well as action:

> Perhaps no passage in the NT [Matthew 7:21–23] expresses more concisely and more sharply that the essence of discipleship, and hence participation in the kingdom, is found not in words,

> nor in religiosity, nor even in the performance of spectacular deeds in the name of Jesus, but only in the manifestation of true righteousness—*i.e.,* the doing of the will of the Father as now interpreted through the teaching of Jesus. Relationship with Jesus is impossible apart from doing the will of God.[28]

The false prophets, the foolish bridesmaids, and the unfaithful servant all have one thing in common: They were unknown to God in terms of election. One can attempt to ignore this estrangement by substituting good works for faith in Christ or—as in the case of the unfaithful servant—to justify it by accusing God of being unfair and thus misrepresenting who God is (25:24–25). What we learn from the unfaithful servant is that grace has a demand, which leaves us with the sobering truth that lack of faithful discipleship provides "proof that a person has not accepted the invitation to accept Christ as Savior, for they refuse to follow Him as Lord."[29]

When sharing a parable, Jesus had a way of capturing the interest of listeners so that they related to what He was saying and probably envisioned how the story would end. But He also had the knack of turning expected endings on their head. The listeners to the Parable of the Talents would

---

28 Donald A. Hagner, *Matthew 1–13* (Dallas, TX: Word Books, 1993), 188; Luke 6:46 reads as an indictment, "Why do you call me, 'Lord, Lord,' and do not do what I say?"

29 Wilkins, *Matthew,* 813.

have expected the master to punish the third servant. But what was shocking was Jesus' pronouncement that lack of production was sufficient evidence for condemnation to eternal punishment. Such an outcome would have been unexpected by all concerned—both then and now![30]

God unleashed His power and wisdom in the cross (1 Corinthians 1:24). He defeated Satan (Colossians 2:15) and established the new creation (2 Corinthians 5:17). The new life in Christ is where we live our discipleship, and the Parable of the Talents lays the groundwork for seeing this. The faithful servants are empowered by God as He allocates the responsibilities to be addressed in their secondary callings; more so, such an allocation, such an investment must produce a return. Taking advantage of such grace, our Lord customizes what we are to do. Discipleship comes in all shapes and sizes, and the final appraisal of our work is simply whether we have "faithfully discharged our responsibilities as disciples, whether they have been small or great. It is the master who allocates the scale of responsibility; the slave's duty is merely to carry out faithfully the role entrusted to him."[31]

---

30 The disciples may have wanted to dig deeper into the meaning of this parable but with the awareness that when they discovered all that Jesus was saying, they probably weren't going to like it.

31 France, *Matthew*, 353.

THREE

Amazing Grace

American surgeon Richard Selzer (1928–2016) shares a moving experience in a postoperative room with a wife who had a tumor removed from her cheek. Selzer did everything he could, but in the end he had to cut a little nerve, thus rendering her lips permanently twisted. Then Selzer shares:

> Her young husband is in the room. He stands on the opposite side of the bed and together they seem to dwell in the evening lamplight, isolated from me, private. *Who are they,* I ask myself, *he and this wry mouth I have made, who gaze at and touch each other so generously, greedily?*
>
> The young woman speaks.
>
> "Will my mouth always be like this?" she asks.
>
> "Yes," I say, "it will. It is because the nerve was cut." She nods and is silent. But the young man smiles.

> "I like it," he says. "It is kind of cute."
>
> All at once, I know who he is. I understand, and I lower my gaze. One is not bold in an encounter with a god. Unmindful, he bends to kiss her crooked mouth, and I am so close I can see how he twists his own lips to accommodate to hers, to show her that their kiss still works.[32]

I read of this incident many years ago but always return to it when trying to imagine what God has done in coming to us in grace: He kisses our crooked lips.

The three dimensions of grace—salvation, transformation, and service—are critical to the correct understanding of our call, our work, and our identity. God is using us, His Easter people, to show the world that the new creation is here, and the undeniable proof is our changed lives. God uses us with our flaws and failures because we have heard His call and follow His Son in discipleship. By the power of the resurrection of His Son, we seek to be the holy people through whom God extends His call to a lost and hopeless world. Paul knew to whom He belonged (Acts 27:23), and this gave him his identity in Christ, for he says, "You died, and your life is now hidden with Christ in God. When Christ, who is your life, appears, then you also will appear with him in glory" (Colossians 3:3–4). We can say we are in Christ, experiencing a "living union through the Holy Spirit, by which we, by faith,

---

32 Richard Selzer, *Mortal Lessons: Notes on the Art of Surgery First Edition* (Orlando, FL: Harcourt, Inc. 1996), 45–46.

draw upon the nourishment and power of the living Christ to enable us to live the Christian life."[33] Such an unbelievable reality is the product of grace.

We Are Saved by Amazing Grace

To confess that we are saved by grace is to state the obvious, but in doing so it is easy to become indifferent and unappreciative of such an overwhelming act of God. The term *salvation* can so easily roll off our lips that we fail to dig deeper to see what it means and how it is meant to be the beginning of our walk with Christ instead of a reason to undervalue it. Such is a major reason we limit the concept of grace to a "one and done" level. However, even our brief look here at the immeasurable result of our salvation should place us wholly into God's debt for the rest of eternity.

The "God of all grace" (1 Peter 5:10) freely shows us mercy and love (Romans 9:15; Exodus 33:19). Such action is necessary because we are unable to earn favor or acceptance regarding God; there is nothing we can do to warrant becoming children of God except to receive this grace by faith, which says we throw ourselves completely on the mercy of God. We are entirely dependent on His grace. Faith excludes dependence on one's own work or merit.

When we come to Christ in faith, we acknowledge His death is sufficient for the atonement for our sins

---

33 Jerry Bridges, *Who Am I?: Identity in Christ* (Adelphi, Maryland: Cruciform Press, 2012), 26.

(Hebrews 9:26). This is the gospel. We were destined for God's wrath (Ephesians 2:3) but have been made alive with Christ (2:5). We live in union with the One who rose from the dead. God has raised us up, and we are seated with Christ at the right hand of the Father, having been made alive with Him and placed in the position to receive the "incomparable riches of His grace" (2:6–7).

God's grace has always been ours. In fact, He blessed us with innumerable blessings before we came to know Him (this is called common grace, Matthew 5:45). And having accepted His Son as Savior, we discover all it means for us to be able to become a disciple. When looking at what it means to be a Christian, we can quickly gain an overview of the grace of salvation by examining what theologians call the "order of salvation" (*ordo salutis*). While many of these components happen instantaneously, the listing follows a logical sequence. Paul provides us with the foundation of what is ours in light of what God did in Christ:

> For those God foreknew he also predestined to be conformed to the image of his Son, that he might be the firstborn among many brothers and sisters. And those he predestined, he also called; those he called, he also justified; those he justified, he also glorified. (Romans 8:29–30)

The events listed in these verses give us the basic picture of what our initial salvation entails. Scripture provides other steps in the process, but essentially "these are the series of events we can expect to witness and experience according to God's design of salvation for someone who has heard and put his or her faith in Jesus Christ."[34]

Our salvation is no accident; it is based purely and solely on the good pleasure of God, for in His sovereignty He chooses us:

> For he chose us in him before the creation of the world to be holy and blameless in his sight. In love he predestined us for adoption to sonship through Jesus Christ, in accordance with his pleasure and will—to the *praise of his glorious grace*, which he has freely given us in the One he loves. (Ephesians 1:4–6; emphasis added)

The first element of God's salvific work is *election*, which took place prior to creation. By election I mean the free act of God choosing us to be saved. Although the idea of God choosing or electing those who are saved is a great mystery, we all can take away the truth that God chose us; we did not choose Him (John 15:16). And such choosing was made with much expectation:

> For this very reason, make every effort to add to your faith goodness; and to

34 Stephen Um, "The Order of Salvation," accessed November 9, 2020, <https://www.thegospelcoalition.org/essay/the-order-of-salvation/>.

> goodness, knowledge; and to knowledge, self-control; and to self-control, perseverance; and to perseverance, godliness; and to godliness, mutual affection; and to mutual affection, love. For if you possess these qualities in increasing measure, they will keep you from being ineffective and unproductive in your knowledge of our Lord Jesus Christ. But whoever does not have them is nearsighted and blind, forgetting that they have been cleansed from their past sins. *Therefore, my brothers and sisters, make every effort to confirm your calling and election.* For if you do these things, you will never stumble, and you will receive a rich welcome into the eternal kingdom of our Lord and Savior Jesus Christ. (2 Peter 1:5–11; emphasis added)

When God elects, He does so expecting a life of obedience and holiness.

The God who chose us extends that invitation to us through the *call*, the second step of salvation. We hear the call of God through the gospel. Some have designated this call the effectual call because those who hear it respond in saving faith, in contrast to those who do not respond. In general, the good news goes out to all, as seen in the Parable of the Sower (Matthew 13:1–9,18–23). This message expresses the need to repent of one's sins, ask for forgiveness, and by faith accept Christ as Savior. But only a few respond (22:14). This message is often rejected by many, but by the Father's gracious will is effective in those who respond with faith (John 6:44). When the good news was shared with us, we accepted the power that can bring about our salvation (Romans 1:16). The gospel is God's personal invitation to respond to His offer of salvation and fulfillment. He reaches out to the whole person:

> He speaks to our intellects by explaining the facts of salvation in his Word. He speaks to our emotions by issuing a heartfelt personal invitation to respond. He speaks to our wills by asking us to hear his invitation and respond willingly in repentance and faith—to decide to turn from our sins and receive Christ as Savior and rest our hearts in him for salvation.[35]

The call is God's summons that results in some people turning to Him and accepting His grace. It is an effectual call because those He elects turn to Him. But simply hearing the gospel is not enough; we are powerless to respond on our own.

"How can a person who is dead in trespasses and sins, whose mind is enmity against God, and who cannot do

35 Grudem, *Systematic Theology*, 696.

that which is well-pleasing to God answer a call to the fellowship of Christ?"[36] When the effectual calling is working in our lives, the Holy Spirit will renovate our hearts so that we are able to receive God's grace and all that He has in store for us (Ezekiel 36:26). This act of renewal is designated *regeneration,* and this third element of salvation signifies what happens when the Holy Spirit imparts new life in us: We are born again, a truth to which Nicodemus was blind (John 3:3–8). This is a mysterious act of the Holy Spirit that must take place before we can believe in Christ. Without being regenerated by the Holy Spirit, we are unable to respond to the call of the gospel. The God who elects us and calls to us must create a new heart in us in order to respond to what He has done for us.

We are passive in this new birth, just as we were in our natural birth. The moment of our spiritual birth may even catch us unawares.[37] But no matter the details of when we were renewed by the Holy Spirit, there should be evidence of a change in us. We now love God, have assurance of salvation, and desire to walk in the Spirit. Over time, there should be proof of a Christlike love for all, a love for God's Word, and a pattern of following Christ in obedience and avoiding a life indulging in sin. We will grow in faith

---

36 John Murray, *Redemption Accomplished and Applied* (Grand Rapids: Eerdmans Publishing, 2015), 99.

37 Such was the case of C. S. Lewis, who relates how one day he left for a trip to a zoo not believing Jesus was the Son of God, only to arrive at the zoo and discover he did. C. S. Lewis, *Surprised by Joy* (San Francisco, CA: HarperOne, 2017), 290.

(Habakkuk 2:4) and in an awareness of sin, coming to the realization that sin is more than simply breaking God's laws; it is the breaking of His heart!

The grace of God is experienced in the context of demand. If the Holy Spirit has entered our life, we should be different, new creations (2 Corinthians 5:17), with different goals and aspirations than before our change of heart. This demand is for our own good, for evidence of change is affirmation that we are on the road to conforming to the image of God we were created to be (Romans 8:29–30). Such change was missing in the third servant of the Parable of the Talents (Matthew 25:14–30), as well as the false disciples (7:21–23). Those truly regenerated will exhibit evidence of rebirth, but not simply in observable deeds; they will have developed a humble heart and a willingness to live in obedience to all of Jesus' commands. This is the proof of a genuine rebirth; this is the core of the disciple worthy of praise.

Accompanying our new birth is *conversion*—our willing response to the gospel call—resulting in faith, the turning *to* Christ for salvation and repentance, the turning *away* from sin (2 Corinthians 7:9–10). Thus, conversion is the moment we believe and repent. Our faith results in repentance:

> For repentance is a fruit of faith, which is itself a fruit of regeneration . . . for repentance is inseparable from faith . . . The idea that there can be saving faith without

> repentance, and that one can be justified by embracing Christ as Savior while refusing him as Lord, is a destructive delusion.[38]

Conversion, the fourth element of salvation, marks our initial encounter with God and His offer of salvation in Christ. The effectiveness of this gracious act will deepen as we realize that coming to God is more than receiving forgiveness that leads to eternal life; the blessings of salvation go beyond our comprehension at this point, for they impact the rest of our life on earth. Conversion is the starting point for a personal relationship with God that grows and then culminates when we receive our resurrected bodies and reign with God forever (1 Corinthians 15:42–44, 49; Matthew 13:43).

I do not want to gloss over the personal nature of the relationship that begins at conversion. The idea of biblical faith reflects trust, for "we can 'believe' something to be true with no personal commitment or dependence involved in it."[39] Most of the world believes that Jesus died on the cross, but few believe that death is relevant to their lives. For many, faith in Christ's atonement is an *irrational* commitment to something that may give you relief, if only to dull the pain of the emptiness of this world. But it is without proof and clearly not worth determining how one should live his or

---

38 J. I. Packer, *Concise Theology* (Carol Stream, IL: Tyndale House Publishers, 2011), 163.

39 Grudem, *Systematic Theology*, 710–711.

her life. It is only when we relate the significance of that death to our helpless situation before God and place our trust in Jesus as Savior that we escape the worldly malaise that comes from the futility of seeking meaning from life apart from God.

John may have had this in mind when he recorded John 3:16. The apostle did not write that eternal life is for those "who believe Jesus," but those "who believe *in* him." This difference gives "the sense of trust or confidence that goes *into* and rests *in* Jesus as a person."[40] The decision to place my trust in Christ as *my* Savior and to follow Him as *my* Lord involves "my heart, the central faculty of my entire being that makes commitments for me as a whole person."[41] Trust is at the core of conversion, a personal act that depends on God, not us.

What logically, though not temporally, follows conversion is *justification*, the fifth element in our look at salvation, and the one which expresses the idea of God's grace as much as any other term. Justification is God's legal declaration that we are forgiven and now counted as having Christ's righteousness (2 Corinthians 5:21); hence, we are declared righteous in God's sight (Romans 3:24, 26). The vividness of this truth is revealed in 5:8, "*But God* demonstrates his own love for us in this: While we were still sinners, Christ died for us" (emphasis added). The conjunction *but* alerts us that a dark and desperate situation is about to change for

---

40 Grudem, *Systematic Theology*, 711.

41 Grudem, *Systematic Theology*, 712.

the better. The words *but God* remind us of the "relentless, merciful intervention of God."[42]

We were powerless and ungodly (5:6), sinners (5:8), and enemies of God (5:9). We should never become comfortable with the truth that we were destined for God's wrath only to be reconciled to Him through Christ's death, that we might be saved through Him (5:10). We must accept that our sin is grievous and offensive to God, for His holiness requires a holy reaction to sin, namely His wrath. Opposition exists on both sides, for "there is not only a wicked opposition of the sinner to God, but a holy opposition of God to the sinner."[43] And yet, God demonstrates His love (present tense) as the cross continues to reveal God's grace and rescue us in our daily walk with Him. Justification results in us being treated as friends and not enemies of God. We can begin to see the wonder of grace in the realization of the extent of our sinfulness, for we realize "that the gospel only produces a full sense of that wonder when we have learned why it is so necessary and are conscious of the terrible realities from which Christ came to save us."[44] These words capture the heart of the disciple praised by Christ.

The concept of justification is one of the greatest doctrines of the Church. What we have is "justification by

---

42 Lute, *But God*, 6.

43 Charles H. Hodge, *A Commentary of Romans* (Crossway Books Wheaton, IL, 1993), 134.

44 Sinclair Ferguson, "Preach Like Hell Lasts Forever," February 29, 2020, accessed February 8, 2021, <https://www.desiringgod.org /articles/preach-like-hell-lastsforever>.

grace through faith," a key doctrine of the Reformation, for salvation by grace alone (*sola gratia*) can be ours only by faith alone (*sola fide*) in Christ alone (*solus Christus*). We find salvation in grace alone when we accept it by faith alone. All this is grace, a gift from the God who elects us, calls us, regenerates us, converts us, and—most significantly—justifies us.

This wonder deepens when we learn that the outcome of justification is the sixth component of salvation, namely our *adoption* into His family:

> For those who are led by the Spirit of God are the children of God. The Spirit you received does not make you slaves, so that you live in fear again; rather, the Spirit you received brought about your adoption to sonship. And by him we cry, "*Abba*, Father." The Spirit himself testifies with our spirit that we are God's children. (Romans 8:14–16)

One of the great privileges of grace is that we can relate to God as a Father. He has adopted us into His family. We are His children, His sons and daughters, as well as Christ's brothers and sisters: "For both the One who sanctifies and those who are sanctified are of the same family. So Jesus is not ashamed to call them brothers" (Hebrews 2:11). The Father loves us (1 John 3:1), meets our needs (Matthew 6:32), and gives us good gifts (7:11).

The idea of giving us gifts reminds us of what becomes ours when God invests His wealth in us (25:14–30). The greatest gift, though, is Himself. We have the right to call Him *Abba*, the Aramaic term used to describe the intimacy between a father and his children. This is not an entitlement since the concept of the universal Fatherhood of God (Acts 17:28–29) was declared null and void with Adam's sin. God seeks us not because He is our Father, but because He desires to become our Father.[45] "The whole gospel is contained in that one little word, *Abba*."[46]

Our goal should now be to honor our Father in all we do (Matthew 5:16). He is the One we live for (1 Corinthians 8:6), pray to (Matthew 6:9), and imitate (Ephesians 5:1). Furthermore, the Father desires that we do "family work" with other children in His family, our brothers and sisters in Christ. We are individual members of one body (1 Corinthians 12:12–13), and our goal is to work together to live out God's will on earth as it is in heaven (Matthew 6:10). When we pray the Lord's prayer (6:9–13), we use the term "our" to remind us we are one body, the bride of Christ (Revelation 21:2). We have a new identity (Galatians 4:6–7) and are recipients of God's love on par with His love for the Son (Romans 8:17). We will

45 George E. Ladd, *A Theology of the New Testament* (Grand Rapids, MI: Eerdmans, 1974), 86.

46 Michael Green, *The Message of Matthew: The Bible Speaks Today* (Downers Grove, IL, 2000), 100.

realize fully the extent of the wonders of our adoption at the resurrection of our bodies (8:23).

The seventh component of our salvation is *sanctification,* the action of God setting us apart for Himself. That is, we are made holy: "You were washed, you were sanctified, you were justified in the name of the Lord Jesus Christ and by the Spirit of our God" (1 Corinthians 6:11). God declares us holy when we accept His offer of salvation. The holiness of Christ *becomes our* holiness, for all Christians are sanctified (Acts 20:32). By accepting Christ as Savior, we have made a break with sin; as a result, we must consider ourselves dead to sin and free from its dominance (Romans 6:11, 18).

The nature of sanctification is twofold. In one sense, it is a one-time event and brings to a close the action of God at our initial salvation. As a result of our conversion, we have taken on a new morality, a new desire to live holy lives. We have been made holy in Christ Jesus and attained the status or position of salt and light. This concept of *positional sanctification* is all of God's doing. Taken in combination with the terms discussed above, God comes to us and performs undeserved acts of kindness and mercy, culminating in declaring us righteous and holy; all this is simply received by faith in Christ. But unlike the other elements in salvation—election through adoption—sanctification also becomes a process whereby we cooperate with God to progress toward becoming like Christ in our daily walk, in our discipleship. In other words, we seek to cooperate with the Holy Spirit, who transforms us into the person God desires.

For our discussion here, we need to recall our exploration of the indicative/imperative (see chapter one): We have been made holy (indicative), now let us live like holy people (imperative), for God's command to us is "Be holy, because I am holy" (1 Peter 1:16). We have been given the new status of positional sanctification—set aside for God's use—and yet, at the same time, our goal is to grow in sanctification (*progressive sanctification*), a dedicated life of discipleship to live out our primary calling in our secondary callings.

The idea of transformation lies at the root of the praiseworthy disciple, both in terms of grace and demand. Such a re-creation is a gift of God, yet it comes with high expectations. We should be compelled to allow the Spirit to free us from the influence of sin, so that we conform to the image of Christ. As we grow in holiness or godliness, we come to realize that our progress is "Holy Spirit dependent,"[47] a working out of what God has done and will continue to do if we cooperate with Him (Philippians 2:12–13). We will never arrive at a sinless life in our time on earth, but as the saying goes, "Though I will never be sinless, nevertheless I should sin less." As we live for God, we await the resurrection of our bodies in perfection; complete sanctification awaits our eternal home.

At first glance, to experience God's grace in terms of justification and positional sanctification seems out of touch with our walk with Christ. We will never love God

---

47 John Murray, *Redemption Accomplished and Applied*, 156–157.

with everything or our neighbor as ourselves, let alone have a pure motive for anything we do. We have all sinned and continue to fall short of God's glory (Romans 3:23) as we grieve the Holy Spirit (Ephesians 4:30) and quench His work (1 Thessalonians 5:19). We see the paradox of being declared holy yet having to strive to live holy lives in Hebrews 10. Here we read that the death of Christ "has made us holy" (10:10), and we will live in His power as "we are made holy" (10:14). In both cases, we are acted on by the Holy Spirit. Why would a holy God accept me, one so unholy? This is the beauty of grace.

Our progress in holy living involves the work of the Holy Spirit at all levels; He must act on us, profoundly changing our will to do what God demands of us as He provides the strength to do so (Philippians 2:12–13). Our role in living a holy life is both passive and active; we both accept the holiness of Christ and cooperate with the Spirit to grow in Christ. We trust in what God has done, yielding to the Spirit, and intentionally working to put ourselves in position to mature in Christ. This is the relentless demand to be the salt and the light in everyday life (Matthew 5:13–16). This growth in holiness is fittingly designated progressive sanctification. And unless "the Spirit and the Word are partners in the enterprise of holiness," we will struggle to reach our potential as disciples.[48]

We cannot succeed in this struggle without a deep appreciation for God's Word. We are to delight in His Word

---

48 Derek Tidball, *The Message of Holiness: The Bible Speaks Today* (Downers Grove: InterVarsity Press, 2010), 133.

and meditate on it (Psalm 1:2). That is, we are to allow the Bible to capture our hearts as we come to treasure God's words: "How sweet are your words to my taste, sweeter than honey to my mouth!" (119:103). This is a conviction, not a feeling. God teaches us personally (119:102) and leads us in purity (119:9). The Word must be hidden in our hearts so that we do not sin (119:11). When discipleship wears us down, we can cry to God, "My soul is weary with sorrow; strengthen me according to your word" (119:28).[49] As we follow His Word, He sets us free (119:32) and steers us away from idols (119:37). He hears our struggles to live holy lives: "Oh, that my ways were steadfast in obeying your decrees! Then I would not be put to shame when I consider all your commands" (119:5–6). His Word "is a lamp for my feet, a light on my path" (119:105). In other words, we strive toward perfection, cognizant of the fact that we will never attain it in this life, only in the next when we reach the grace of perfection. But before we reach that state, we are to progress in our holiness and relentlessly strive to become more like Christ. By living a life of determined discipleship, we will remain faithful, from the time of our conversion until our death; such faithfulness is the concept of *perseverance*, our eighth element in the order of salvation.

The concept of perseverance of the saints (eternal security; once saved always saved) has long been a battleground for believers. In other words, perseverance is God's gift that

49 While our Lord speaks to us in His Word, we speak to Him through the Psalms.

results in "continual belief and on-going transformation in a believer's life."[50] We see strong biblical evidence that those who are truly born again (truly regenerated) will be protected by God's power and will continue (persevere) in the faith until the end of their lives.

Jesus promises that He will not lose any of those the Father has given Him (John 6:39) and that no one can snatch His sheep from His hand (10:28–29). In both instances, the people will receive eternal life (6:40; 10:28). In fact, Paul is so certain that those who sincerely believe in Christ will be glorified that he speaks of that future event as already taking place: "And those he predestined, he also called; those he called, he also justified; those he justified, he also glorified" (Romans 8:30). The Holy Spirit seals us:

> And you also were included in Christ when you heard the message of truth, the gospel of your salvation. When you believed, you were marked in him with a seal, the promised Holy Spirit, who is a deposit guaranteeing our inheritance until the redemption of those who are God's possession—to the praise of his glory. (Ephesians 1:13–14)

By granting us the Holy Spirit, God guarantees our salvation, for He is committed to rewarding faithful disciples with life eternal.

---

50 Um, "The Order of Salvation."

But the balance to the teaching of eternal security is that only those who persevere until the end have truly been born again. That is, there should be clear evidence in a disciple that shows sustained trust in Christ for salvation, namely the fruit of the Spirit (Galatians 5:22–23), continued holding to sound church doctrine and love of the saints, and persistent—even tenacious—growth in Christ (2 Peter 1:5–9). This is where commitment is so important. Our Christian walk should affirm our election and calling (1:10–11), for we are called to a discipleship that results in obedience and holiness (1 Peter 1:2; Ephesians 1:3–6).

Paul's confidence in the continued protection of God is clearly expressed when he writes "that he who began a good work in you will carry it on to completion until the day of Christ Jesus" (Philippians 1:6). From our election until we receive our resurrection bodies, the grace of God guards us and sustains us. The grace of God demands much of us, but our effort is merged into the power and action of God:

> This God-dependent effort that is enabled by grace is also sustained by that same grace. This work of continual belief and ongoing transformation in a believer's life is commonly referred to as God's gift of perseverance. We are able to persevere through various trials of faith because of our God who holds onto us, who promises to deliver us from the beginning to the end without quitting on us.[51]

---

51 Um, "The Order of Salvation."

As we progress in our sanctification, in our growth in holiness, we will face many trials and temptations. Our faith and our walk with God will be challenged, but Christ promises us that "the one who stands firm [perseveres] to the end will be saved" (Matthew 24:13). This promise can be trusted because the One who made it will always be with those who are His (28:20). "The application of God's salvation begins with grace, is sustained through grace, and will be completed by grace."[52] Such grace to remain faithful to God safeguards our final destination.

The perseverance provided by God brings us to the final element of salvation, our *glorification*. This is not referring to our death and when we enter the intermediate state of being in the presence of Christ (Philippians 1:23). While this is glorious in and of itself, we will be in the period between leaving our present bodies and receiving our resurrected bodies. We were created to have bodies and hence glorification is our complete and final salvation, when we receive our new bodies and the earth is recreated. Christ "will transform our lowly bodies so that they will be like His glorious body" (3:21) and "creation itself will be liberated from its bondage to decay and brought into the freedom and glory of the children of God" (Romans 8:21). We are recreated to fully bear the image and likeness of Christ (8:29). This glorious time follows Christ's return (1 Thessalonians 4:13–18).

---

52 Um, "The Order of Salvation."

The hope of a new earth and freedom from sin, death, struggle, pain, racism, and oppression should always be in our thinking (Revelation 21:1–4). Salvation begins and ends with God. From our election until our glorification, God provides help and fellowship—with His people and with Himself. While election occurred before the world was created, our call through our positional sanctification essentially occurred when we became a Christian. We have briefly examined these elements in logical fashion, though there is really no timeline; they are instantaneous. Once these components become a reality in our lives, we begin the process of discipleship, of living our primary call in our everyday secondary callings. We are to progress in our sanctification, persevering until the day we meet Christ face-to-face in anticipation of our glorification.

We must not fail to see the magnitude of what our initial salvation involves. Yet we must be careful not to restrict its impact and importance to the early days of our Christian life. While these elements describe what happens when we accept Christ as Savior, these one-time events have continuing influence throughout our lives. We live by faith and will regularly repent; the impact of our regeneration continues in our walk with the Holy Spirit; our legal standing stemming from justification remains intact; and we will always be a member of God's family. These terms, so easily referred to, should cause us to bow in humility and thankfulness because of the tremendous price paid for our salvation and the even greater potential for our enjoying the Godhead for eternity. These truths:

> ought to give us confidence and assurance of our salvation. In times of doubts, struggles, and hardships when we are tempted to doubt God's presence and faithfulness in our lives, we are called to remember who God is and all that he's done. Remembering this is not simply a mental exercise but the experience of the Holy Spirit at work within us, carrying us through the highs and lows of our spiritual journeys.[53]

Grace Is a Terrible Thing to Waste

Before examining the demands that accompany our salvation, we must confront a disturbing possibility. The logical conclusion to salvation by faith is a changed life, a recreated disciple. But such is not always the case, as noted by Paul in his second letter to the Corinthians. Following his masterful description of the message of reconciliation (5:18–21), Paul cautions, "As God's fellow workers, then, we urge you not to receive God's grace in vain" (6:1), not to see such grace wasted. The desired results for which God saved us is that we grow in Christlikeness. Paul assumes that they have received the gospel, for they are ambassadors of reconciliation and coworkers with him. But it appears that though

53 Um, "The Order of Salvation."

some had learned that Jesus died for them, they "had not yet died to themselves."[54]

We will have full and perfect fellowship with God in the next life; shouldn't we seek to enjoy such fellowship as much as we can in this life? We must be aware that the words "Follow Me" entail much more than salvation from hell. Such grace has a demand. As we accept what Christ did for us, we must take up our cross daily and lose our life for His cause (Luke 9:23–25). We must not cheapen grace by accepting Christ's death on the cross and then not pursuing a holy lifestyle, as Paul warns. We must avoid the temptation to receive the grace of God without changing our desires and action. This signals an "easy-believism."

Grace informs us of what we are saved *from;* but we should be equally aware of what we are saved *for.* It is a dangerous position to say, "I have accepted Jesus as Savior but not as Lord." Good works as a believer do nothing for our salvation, but they offer evidence that we "walk as Jesus did" (1 John 2:6). As James reminds us, obedience is a requirement to demonstrate that faith is real (2.17). Paul warns that we all must stand before the judgment seat of Christ to receive our due for how we have performed as a disciple (2 Corinthians 5:10). Some will hear the precious words, "Well done, now enter your Master's happiness"; others will "barely escape destruction" (1 Corinthians 3;10–15). Thus, to downplay the need for transformation is dangerous. It

---

54 Ralph Martin, *2 Corinthians. Vol. 40 Word Biblical Commentary* (Waco, TX: Word Books, 1986), 166.

has been called "eternity's tragedy—[which is] the frustration of grace . . . When God gives men all His grace and they take their own foolish way and frustrate that grace which might have recreated them, once again Christ is crucified and the heart of God is broken."[55]

But which is the greater tragedy? To never hear the message of grace or to hear and presume on its riches, as though its recreative powers are already a reality? We must realize that "salvation is a present possession whose riches [we] may and must explore and enjoy, day after day."[56] Nothing is wrong with expecting an intimate relationship with God as a reward for our faithfulness. But grace is its own reward, and only when it radiates through all we do and think can we come close to what God desires for us. We must allow the Holy Spirit to dominate our body, mind, and soul so that the already-accomplished work of Christ's salvation can be realized in those who live in Him in faithful discipleship.

---

55 William Barclay, *The Letters to the Corinthians: The Daily Bible Study* (Philadelphia: Westminster Press, 1975), 211–212.

56 J. A. Motyer, *The Message of Philippians: The Bible Speaks Today* (Downers Grove: InterVarsity Press, 1991), 83.

FOUR

Under New Management

When asked to perform a wedding, I require premarital counseling. The first words out of my mouth in the opening session are, "I want to address two misunderstandings about successful and flourishing marriages. First, such marriages are not an accident; you do not get lucky and find the right person and then live happily ever after. You must work hard to be the right person. Second, you don't have to be a rocket scientist to know what to do: Just read your vows." During the wedding ceremony, the woman and the man pledge their undying devotion and loyalty to each other no matter what. But such promises—though well intended—are far from reality at this point. The couple pledge to forsake all others and devote their lives, thoughts, and hearts to the one they marry. But it will take more than simple desire and emotion to produce a fulfilling marriage. It will take great effort and willingness to change as they begin the day-to-day routine of living out their love in the holy bonds of matrimony.

In a similar way, we seek to live under the lordship of Jesus Christ. We accept Him as Savior and instantaneously are part of His family. At our conversion, we pledge our undying love for Him and promise to follow Him in discipleship. We declare Him Lord of our lives, not really understanding what all that entails. To accept Christ as Lord (*kýrios,* the equivalent of the Old Testament term *Yahweh*) is to deed ownership of our life over to Him. The earliest Christian confession was "Jesus Christ is Lord"; there is no other title more appropriate for Him regarding our discipleship. He is the final authority and power in our Christian walk, and we must never view His lordship as an option or allow the term *Lord* to roll off our lips thoughtlessly.

The manner in which the lordship of Christ becomes a reality in our lives is similar to the growth in a marriage between a husband and wife. When we profess Jesus as Lord, we should start on a journey of progressive sanctification, one that is characterized by a deep-seated change. As we seek to blend our lives with that of our spouse so that the "two will become one flesh" (Ephesians 5:31), we seek to walk with Christ in order to become one with Him: "For if we have been united with him like this in his death, we will certainly also be united with him in his resurrection" (Romans 6:5). In both cases, it is one habit, one action at a time that constitutes the transformation. Whether in marriage or walking with Christ, a demand must be met in order for the transformation to take place. It's not a demand in the sense that we are doing anything against our will, but a high standard that requires much effort and time if we want our relationships to thrive. We must be ready, willing, and able to put in the effort both to enable our marriage (a part of our discipleship) and our walk with Christ to reach their full potential.

We Are Transformed by Grace

Earlier I quoted Ephesians 2:8–9, which clearly lays out that we are saved by God's grace. But the following verse expands our understanding of grace when we read, "For we are God's handiwork, created in Christ Jesus . . . " (2:10a). The thought behind *handiwork* or *masterpiece* is centered on our spiritual rebirth or re-creation. We are God's masterpiece, created in Christ to live and act like God, not reject Him like the third servant in the Parable of the Talents. What is in mind here is holy living, embedded in the understanding of sanctification; we are "being set apart for God." We are to be a holy example of the gospel.[57] We are to talk and act differently, living as ones easily distinguished from the world. We are to have clean hands and pure hearts so that we will not fall prey to idolatry (Psalm 24:4). But how can this be? Even as God's masterpieces, many reading this book know the uphill struggle to even come close to living like God's image was intended to live. Our sinful nature makes the beautiful words "well done" appear out of our reach as we strive to be the disciples that receive such a commendation. Yet by God's grace, the necessary change

57 Devotion for March 10 in Oswald Chambers' *My Utmost for His Highest* (Bloomington, MN: Garborg's Heart 'n Home, Inc., 1992).

has been set in motion. As we strive to ensure our marriages are all they can be, we must have the same vision about living for Christ. Any other perception denies the essential element in our pursuit of worthy discipleship, namely *a God-centered desire for holiness*:

> Our desire for holiness, our motivation to pursue it, must be a God-centered desire and motivation. Developing this God-centered motivation requires practice or training; it does not come naturally or easily. We are by nature self-centered. If we are diligent to examine ourselves, we will often find that our motivation is self-centered. We must confess and renounce this, just as we must any disobedient action, and then seek a God-centered motivation.[58]

Part of the beauty and mystery of God's grace is our spiritual prosperity. At salvation we became new creations (2 Corinthians 5:17) and dead to sin (Romans 6:2). Our goal becomes to imitate God (Ephesians 5:1) and seek to live so that we will be holy in all that we do (1 Peter 1:15–16). We should reflect the life of Christ in terms of the fruit of the Spirit (Galatians 5:22–23) and virtues (strengths of character) which reflect Christlike behavior (Colossians 3:12–14). At conversion, our hearts

58 Jerry Bridges, *The Practice of Godliness* (Colorado Springs, CO: Navpress, 1996), 129–130.

and our spirits were reborn by the Holy Spirit in regeneration (Ezekiel 36:26–27), and our wills reshaped to desire to live holy lives (Titus 3:5). The idea of growing in holiness shows that the Spirit transforms us when we cooperate with Him and allow Him to re-create us. To grow in holiness is to become "increasingly God-centered, Christlike and Spirit-empowered."[59]

Through self-discipline, we practice the spiritual disciplines and fight every day for our faith (Colossians 3:10). We read God's Word regularly, fellowship with other believers, and have set times for prayer. These activities are part and parcel of discipleship. As we follow a life of holiness, we put ourselves in a better place to avoid the snares and seductions of the world as we serve God. Discipleship that receives the commendation of Christ is one that both serves others and stands firm in living a life that is pure and consecrated to God (Matthew 5:13–16). Holiness is not an option!

To be transformed into a Christlike disciple is the second aspect of God's grace. The concept of salvation is not limited to our conversion; it is only the beginning, for we are "saved through the sanctifying work of the Spirit" (2 Thessalonians 2:13). Our salvation is actualized in greater degree as we embrace "the fullness of God's purpose to deliver us from the ravages and consequences of sin, culminating in our final, heavenly destiny."[60] In other words, we live out

---

59 Tidball, *The Message of Holiness*, 23.

60 John Stott, *The Message of 1 & 2 Thessalonians: The Bible Speaks Today* (Downers Grove, IL: InterVarsity Press, 1991), 176.

our salvation when we live like the first two servants in the Parable of the Talents. Dedicated discipleship is a life of holiness that displays the wonders of God's grace. But this display is not automatic: It is the result of hard work, of meeting the demand of God in light of His grace.

We accept our salvation by grace but often fail to walk by grace in our day-to-day living. We can misplace the grace available to us by basing "our personal relationship with God on performance instead of on His grace . . . In this sense, we live by works rather than grace."[61] We strive to achieve a life of holiness by trying harder and looking within ourselves to approach perfection. It is almost as if we have forgotten that God's love for us is ours for the taking; we do not have to keep earning it. Such a mindset leads to exhaustion and a self-defeating Christian life, hoping that God will somehow accept us when all is said and done.

Or worse, we may act as some of the Corinthians did, devaluing grace and simply keeping it in our back pocket for when we leave this world. After declaring Jesus as Lord, we simply live like we want to, succumbing to the belief that God's sole reason for existing is to make sure we are happy and comfortable. At times we serve Him so that we can manipulate Him and somehow obtain all we want. As a result, dedicated discipleship becomes less urgent and necessary, and especially less attractive, when our effort is met with opposition or lack of worldly success. We "follow" Jesus to guarantee we will have the good life

61 Bridges, *Transforming Grace*, 11–12.

but reject becoming like Him, which is the essence of the transforming grace of the Holy Spirit. Essentially, we do not allow God's grace to change us because we either do not understand it is our only means of transformation or do not believe we are expected to change.

We must accept that the life of discipleship requires our effort undergirded by God's power and grace; but our effort should be for His glory, not ours. Paul writes, "And you should imitate me, just as I imitate Christ" (1 Corinthians 11:1; NLT). The one who imitates puts out effort in mimicking another. We cannot do this on our own, but we must put forth great effort in cooperating with the Holy Spirit, for we must "strive . . . for the holiness without which no one will see the Lord" (Hebrews 12:14; ESV). To strive is to devote serious effort or energy toward a goal. That is, we must pursue holiness, to relentlessly stalk the life that pleases our Lord. This is a joint venture between God and the Christian. No one can attain any degree of holiness without God working in their life; just as surely, no one will realize it without effort on their part. God has made it possible for us to walk in holiness. "But He has given to us the responsibility of doing the walking; He does not do that for us."[62]

Holiness is reflected in our character, which is composed of habits developed one decision at a time. Holy living is simply developing good habits or "a second nature" which

---

62 Jerry Bridges, *The Pursuit of Holiness* (Colorado Springs, Co.: Navpress, 1996), 9.

reflects choices not characteristic of our first or sinful nature. We must actively seek to "be transformed by the renewing of our mind" (Romans 12:2). In between the declaration that we have been made holy (1 Corinthians 6:11) and the day we will be granted complete holiness (1 Thessalonians 5:23), we are "being transformed into his image with ever-increasing glory, which comes from the Lord, who is the Spirit" (2 Corinthians 3:18).

We live out our holy calling in our daily following of Christ. We hear and follow our primary calling as we live holy lives in our secondary callings. Grace beckons us to be the disciples that will hear "well done." Much cooperation and hard work are needed on our part to utilize the transformative power of grace. However, this will not be achieved simply by outstanding effort. We must be convinced that holy discipleship is the only acceptable way to serve our Lord. And occasional "spikes" on our obedience barometer are not what I am talking about. Rather, we must change our way of thinking and perceiving if we are to take on the "well done" mindset. We must be transformed from within before we can live as we should.

We have already taken the time to examine what God has done for us; we will now look at what He can do in us. We must discover the times and areas of our life where He is working to conform us to the image of His Son, being the disciple who provides great return on God's investment. Such an investment is common to all of Jesus' followers; it remains to be seen how we run "the race marked out for us" (Hebrews 12:1). Our unique traits and character will shape a different looking journey of discipleship from other Christians, but in detail only; the overall direction will be the same, living on the narrow path (Matthew 7:13–14).

As disciples of Christ, it is not that we are the only people of virtue. The understanding of the ancient Greeks as well as the public today is that people should seek to live a virtuous life, a life which seeks to make this world a better place. The "cardinal" virtues of courage, prudence, temperance, and justice are a good place to start. But this is not enough. Early Christians (as well as those reading this book) found out there is more to life than the virtues just mentioned:

> What the earliest Christians were struck by, and what they returned to again and again, was that in Jesus they had seen (and the stories testified of this to those who had not seen) a way of being human which nobody had ever imagined before. This was a way of generosity and forgiveness, a way of self-emptying and a determination to put everyone else's needs first, which was both original in itself and the source of those other virtues that are commonly recognized as Christian innovations—namely, humility, charity, patience [with others and with yourself], and chastity.[63]

63 N. T. Wright, *After You Believe: Why Christian Character Matters* (New York: HarperOne, 2010), 131.

Such is the way of discipleship, a life that can be described as meeting the demand of God that we reflect His nature. And by doing so, He graciously establishes the work of our hands (Psalm 90:17).

Breaking Out of the Mold

How does one prepare to progress in holiness? It is not a result of simply wanting to be a faithful follower of Christ. Our achieving good things for God is the result of our overall striving to live holy lives. Paul says it well in Romans 12:1–2, where he provides a roadmap to holiness:

> Therefore, I urge you, brothers and sisters, in view of God's mercy, to offer your bodies as a living sacrifice, holy and pleasing to God—this is your true and proper worship. Do not conform to the pattern of this world but be transformed by the renewing of your mind. Then you will be able to test and approve what God's will is—his good, pleasing and perfect will.

The "therefore" connects our passage to what Paul has been emphasizing in Romans 1–11: We are made righteous by the death of Christ on the cross (3:22); empowered by the Holy Spirit (8:11); and adopted into the family of God (8:16). These are just a few of the many aspects of God's mercy, as we have discussed. In gratitude, we are to offer our bodies as a "living sacrifice." To offer our bodies is to live a holy life that is pleasing to God. The idea of *body* carries with it the idea of the whole person, not just the part of us that is flesh and blood. That is, I am a body rather than I have a body.[64] The use of the term here supports our belief that sanctification reaches to the depths of our being. Thus, our physical body, spirit, mind, and emotions are to be set apart for God. Such an offering is "an act of intelligent worship" (12:1; PHILLIPS), for what we do is logical in light of the mercies of God and rational in that our worship must include our minds.[65]

Offering our bodies in holiness is an act of presenting a witness for Christ that is both different (salt) and visible (light). This is what is called "authentic Christian discipleship."[66] It is the concrete actions that people see—what we do (or don't do) in the body—that show whose we are and the way people ought to live. The discipleship that Christ demands of His people will be one where:

> Our feet will walk in his paths, our lips will speak the truth and spread the gospel, our tongues will bring healing, our hands will lift up those who have fallen, and perform many mundane tasks as well like

---

64 Rudolf Bultmann, *Theology of the New Testament* (Waco, TX: Baylor University Press, 2007), 192.

65 John Stott, *The Message of Romans: The Bible Speaks Today* (Downers Grove: InterVarsity Press, 1994), 321.

66 Stott, *The Message of Romans*, 322.

> cooking and cleaning, typing and mending; our arms will embrace the lonely and the unloved, our ears will listen to the cries of the distressed, and our eyes will look humbly and patiently towards God.[67]

This is a difficult picture to think about, let alone act out. But we must consider it in order to position ourselves to be Christ's hands and feet. Most people aspire to do much of what was just mentioned but find themselves powerless to do so, or to do it for the glory to God. We must be His people before we can bring Him glory.

And this all starts with allowing God to transform our minds, which is the first step in our striving to live as holy people. By mind (*nous*) is meant our thinking power, using our reason to direct our morals and actions. Here we discover what we value and cherish and what principles we live by. It is in our mind that we think, know, and judge what is right and wrong, and act appropriately. In another example of grace, we have the mind of Christ (1 Corinthians 2:16) and thus access to "insight into the very mind of God himself."[68] We must always be guarding our minds (Philippians 4:7). The challenge becomes one of a war against the flesh, for though I know in my mind what I want to do, my sinful tendencies push me in the wrong direction (Romans 7:13–25). To be conformed and

67 Stott, *The Message of Romans*, 322.

68 Ladd, *A Theology of the New Testament*, 476.

transformed are verbs in the passive voice, showing that in both instances we are acted upon. J.B. Phillips' famous paraphrase of the first half of 12:2 says it well: "Don't let the world around you squeeze you into its own mold but let God re-mold your minds from within." These twin ideas of do not conform/but be transformed are designated as "Paul's version of the call to nonconformity and to holiness, which is addressed to the people of God throughout Scripture."[69]

The call to be transformed (*metamorphoō*) is a directive to be repeated daily. The verb is used at Jesus' transfiguration (Mark 9:2), and, though the disciples present were privy to an outward change, such alteration was simply the reflection of who Jesus is. Our inward change is in progress, as the Holy Spirit seeks to reform our minds and wills, fruits of regeneration. We are to allow the Spirit and the Word to change our thinking and compel us to "to live as saints." Day by day, thought by thought, we are to allow the Holy Spirit to place in our minds what God wants from us:

> Finally, brothers, whatever is true, whatever is honorable, whatever is right, whatever is pure, whatever is lovely, whatever is admirable—if anything is excellent or praiseworthy—think on these things. (Philippians 4:8)

---

69 Stott, *The Message of Romans*, 322.

Considering God's grace, we must live differently than the world. There are only two choices (Matthew 7:13–14).

The world and the Bible present the only two value systems from which to choose, and they are diametrically opposed to each other. When we look at the purpose of life, how to measure greatness, the sanctity of sex, the use of money and power, the potential of humans to make this world a better place, we come away with a clear picture of the demand of God and the practices of those who reject Him. While the world may offer many different answers to the issues just posed, they all fall under the heading of compromise when we are presented with a biblical worldview. The uncompromising demand of God leaves us vulnerable considering the hostility of a nonbelieving world that values the *status quo* and prefers darkness to light (John 3:19).

Despite this, the journey of transformation is a rewarding one, a time of discovery. At conversion, we are regenerated by the power of the Holy Spirit, including our minds, which are then empowered to discern, desire, and determine the will of God. We test its validity and ability to satisfy us by following what God wants, discovering that the Spirit and the Word develop a hunger in us to live for Him (Matthew 5:6); and thus, we become stronger in our walk with God. That is, we "prove in practice that the plan of God for [us] is good, meets all his demands and moves towards the goal of true maturity" (Romans 12:2; PHILLIPS). If we are receptive, this process repeats itself in terms of spiraling upward as our second nature is strengthened. As with our marriage example, one must live out the "wedding vows" daily; the faithfulness and love required for a fulfilling marriage must become our second nature, and this is done only as we honor our pledge and discover confirmation through our actions. In similar fashion, as members of the bride of Christ, we must utilize our spiritual prosperity by cooperating with the Holy Spirit and following the Word of God, so as to not be molded into what the world views as sensible.

What Is Your Elephant?

Many years ago, I designed a course titled "Christianity in a Pluralistic World." I soon discovered that the concept of worldview (in German *weltanschauung*) was critical to providing the needed foundation to teach the course. A worldview is simply a "commitment, a fundamental orientation of the heart" that interprets the events and experiences of life.[70] Through this, we understand the world in a particular manner. Often, we have not taken the trouble to articulate what these beliefs are, and even if we have, we may discover that our actions do not reflect what we really believe.

> Our worldview generally lies so deeply embedded in our subconscious that unless we have reflected long and hard, we are

70 James W. Sire, *The Universe Next Door,* fifth edition (Downers Grove, IL: IVP Academic, 2009), 20.

> unaware of what it is. Even when we think we know what it is and lay it out clearly in neat propositions and clear stories, we may well be wrong. Our actions may belie our self-knowledge.[71]

The worldview we hold is our commitment to what we think is true, and our articulation of that view is what we hold to be our guiding principles.

Everybody has a worldview—whether they are aware of it or not—but close examination of one's beliefs leads to the surprising conclusion that our worldview is fundamentally presuppositional, simply assumptions that we hold to be true. This truth is emphasized in a story shared by James Sire.

> One day a young boy informed his father that his teacher reported the earth was surrounded by space. The boy asked, "How can that be? What holds up the world?" The father replied that "a camel holds up the world, son."
>
> The boy was satisfied with this answer and went away only later to decide that his father's answer was incomplete. The next day he asked, "Dad, what holds up the camel?" Though the father knew this

71 Sire, *The Universe*, 21–22.

> was not going to end well, he quickly responded that "it's a kangaroo that holds up the camel." It was not long afterward that the son asked, "What holds up the kangaroo that holds up the camel?"
>
> With a raised voice the father replied, "It's an elephant that holds up the kangaroo." "Come on, Dad!" the son retorted. "What holds up the elephant?" His dad replied, "It's . . . it's . . . it's the elephant all the way down."[72]

The logic of the father's answer had been pushed to its limits, for his son's questioning required a first holder, something that does not require something to hold it up. This is what is called prime reality, or what is really real.

In mathematics, we have the Commutative Axiom for Addition, where it is assumed true that if you have two numbers x and y, then x + y = y + x. An axiom is an unprovable rule, or first principle accepted as true because it is self-evident. We simply are asked to take it on faith. Likewise, we may believe something is true because it is clearly stated in the Bible. We may believe God to be the author of good and that He has revealed His will in the Bible. But such positions may be camels and kangaroos to skeptics because, when pushed, we can only say, "It's God all the way down."

---

72 James W. Sire, *Naming the Elephant: Worldview as a Concept* (Downers Grove, IL: InterVarsity Press, 2004), 15–16.

The biblical worldview requires such faith, though we have ample reason to testify to its truthfulness. We should be sensitive to another's position and feelings, but confident that all truth is God's truth. We need to think through our beliefs so that we are clear, that we know what we believe and why we believe it to be true. We must not be swayed by what is "trending today." Paul commands us to be deeply rooted in Christ's love so that we will clearly recognize worldviews that deny the love of God as found in Christ and seek simply to domesticate Him, making Him no more than the beloved Mr. Rogers with a beard (Ephesians 3:17–21).

We need to speak the language of the world. Paul could quote from pagan authors (Acts 17:28; 1 Corinthians 15:33; Titus 1:12) to make a point. We do not need to think that there is no truth in non-Christian worldviews, but we must be careful how deep we take in such truth. We want to be knowledgeable of how the world feels and thinks and yet positioned and prepared to point to Christ and all that He has done for us.

This demand to think like this comes at a great cost in today's world. We must be set apart in *our thinking*. We need to be clear in our minds about what we value as priorities and commitments. We should not naively accept the basic assumptions of the world's thinking. The basic overall story—the metanarrative—for us is the biblical narrative that views the overarching, all-embracing story for humanity as accurately described by the "creation-fall-redemption-restoration" paradigm. This fourfold model is the center from which we evaluate all that happens. We must "think Christianly," informing ourselves with what God's grace offers and what His demands require of us to be His disciples. We must be aware of the concerns and vocabulary of the world and seek to inform those around us of the good news of the gospel. Do we miss opportunities because we are unaware of them, or we are not prepared or open to take advantage of them? To live as the salt of the earth is to come out and be separate from the world's thinking.

Peter raises the bar high for articulating our witness in a society which is becoming increasingly hostile to the Christian worldview.

> But in your hearts revere [sanctify] Christ as Lord. Always be prepared to give an answer to everyone who asks you to give the reason for the hope that you have. But do this with gentleness and respect. (1 Peter 3:15)

Those who revere and consider Jesus as their Lord will be prepared to respond to those who want to know why they have hope in a world that is bleak and hopeless. The idea behind the term "answer" (*apologia*) is that of presenting a reasoned explanation for what we believe. Our answer is the result of intense reflection and introspection, where we examine our basic beliefs. We can simply share what Christ means to us. The temptation when we are being grilled because of our faith is to resort to defense mechanisms such as belligerence or name-calling or engaging in point-counterpoint exchanges. We easily become more concerned with winning an argument and saving face than being used by God to penetrate a hard heart. We are to share our witness with gentleness and respect. You will not change a person's mind by personal attacks, but the Spirit can use the irrefutable witness of a changed life to speak to those who are quick to dismiss the gospel as foolishness. We must remember that our faith is reasonable. "Trusting and committing yourself to what you have good reason to think is true and trustworthy, in those cases when doing so is appropriate or unavoidable, is the most reasonable thing you can do."[73]

The hope which Peter speaks of is a "living hope through the resurrection of Jesus Christ from the dead" (1 Peter 1:3), a truth Paul presented to Herod Agrippa and Festus (Acts 26:1–32). Paul asks, "Why would any of you consider it incredible that God raises the dead?" (26:8), a question which eventually leads the procurator Festus to accuse Paul of being "out of his mind" because his great knowledge has driven him insane (26:24). The apostle's response is classic: "I am not insane, most excellent Festus; what I am saying is true and reasonable" (26:25). In other words, Paul was showing that our faith is just as rational and logical as any other worldview. It all starts with our elephant.

---

73 David Horner, *Mind Your Faith* (Downers Grove, IL: InterVarsity Press, 2001), 170.

We are commanded to love God with all of our mind (Mark 12:30). This means we use our reasoning abilities to understand our faith. We follow Anselm (1033–1109), who shows the proper relationship of faith to human reason with the motto: "faith seeking understanding." His prayer is:

> I am not trying, O Lord, to penetrate your loftiness, for I cannot begin to match my understanding with it, but I desire in some measure to understand your truth, which my heart believes and loves. For I do not seek to understand in order to believe, but I believe in order to understand. For this too I believe, that unless I believe, I shall not understand.[74]

He was praying with the mindset that we can understand the things of God only *after* we first believe them. In other words, we use our intellect to comprehend what we already believe.

This truth was reinforced again and again in a course I taught, "Introduction to the Gospels." When we read the Gospel accounts of the resurrection, the students' minds were made up in advance. Either the passage was reporting the truth, or it was a mistranslation or the creative fiction of the gospel writers. The point is that their beginning presup-

---

74 Saint Anselm, *Proslogion*, accessed November 17, 2020, <https://biblestudyforcatholics.com/prayerof-st-anselm>.

position ("their elephant") determined their interpretation of the account. A recurring answer of the skeptics in the class was "I can't believe the resurrection actually happened as reported in the Gospels because the evidence is overwhelmingly against it." What evidence?! Nothing in the resurrection accounts speaks against the bodily resurrection of Christ. But the unwillingness to accept the supernatural prevents some from accepting this truth.

Similarly, when teaching a class on "World Religions," I perceived there was an "elephant in the room." Those skeptical of Christianity clung to the need for empirical, testable evidence to prove assertions. Yet Christianity is set apart from all other religions in that its truthfulness is linked to a "single, testable historical event,"[75] namely the resurrection of Jesus. Other belief systems may point to certain events in history but ultimately, they assert the truthfulness of their worldview to an inner experience or feeling for validity, something that cannot be demonstrated empirically! And such perspectives apply to the naturalistic or atheistic worldview as well. The view of reality that *believes* that matter is all that exists and there is no God is just as much a faith statement as that of Genesis 1:1, "In the beginning God created the heavens and earth." To rely on the scientific method as proof that there is no God requires a major assumption (axiom), namely that this method of

75 Craig Hazen, "Christianity in a World of Religions," in *Passionate Convictions: Contemporary Discourses on Christian Apologetics,* Edited by Paul Copan and William Lane Craig (Nashville, TN: B&H Academic, 2007), 143.

investigation discovers all that is real. But there is no way to prove that is true. So, whether Christian or not, our elephant filters what we want to be true. As Christians we feel vulnerable if we cannot be guaranteed to win every argument about our faith. Often the charge is we are irrational since we cannot offer "proof" of God's existence. If such a fear prevents us from being all-in for discipleship, we have fallen prey to the world and have allowed it to "squeeze us into its mold."

Simply put, we must stake our lives on the truthfulness and trustworthiness of the Bible. Carl F. H. Henry, well-known Evangelical theologian of the twentieth century, bluntly reminds us: "Unless you have confidence that the Bible speaks to everything—politics, economics, alliances and diplomacy, the environment, racial issues—we're sunk; it's over. Go home."[76] Our trust must be in God and His Word. As Paul urged in Romans 12:2, offer your mind to be transformed by experiencing the will of God as it guides and affirms your walk with Him.

You might counter my thinking with the thought that the biblical worldview comes across as politically incorrect, especially when there is no absolute proof for it in the minds of many people. But remember two things. First, no worldview is based primarily on observable facts.

76 Aaron Cline Hanbury, "Seven Questions about Carl F.H. Henry with Gregory Alan Thornbury," *Towers* 12, no. 2 (September 2013): 14–15, accessed November 17, 2020, <https://equip.sbts.edu/publications/towers/sevenquestions-about-carl-f-h-henry-with-gregory-alan-thornbury>.

Every worldview is based on unprovable assumptions; even worldviews that are atheistic in nature must assume ("have faith") that observable data identifies all that exists in the world, both in the physical and nonphysical. But such an assumption cannot be proven. It is one thing for the scientific method to be a means to discover what exists in the physical world, but quite another if it is used to support a great leap by expounding philosophical (metaphysical, "beyond the physical") conclusions about what cannot be discovered through our senses.

Second, certainty is overrated. As Alister McGrath states, "You can be sure that 2 + 2 = 4, but is that going to change your life? Is that going to give you a reason to live and hope in the face of death?"[77] The reality of our faith in God is not diminished because we lack the certainty humans think is necessary to believe something supernatural. Do I believe the resurrection is true simply because of an empty tomb or also because of God's love for me? When all is said and done, the truth of the resurrection begins with love, and then is lived out in faith.[78] We all stand at the foot of the cross to acknowledge the fact that God loves us and has redeemed us at the cost of His only Son. We cannot find God without the cross, and we would not know about the cross except for the resurrection.

---

77 Alister McGrath, "When Doubt Becomes Unbelief," Ligonier Ministries, January 1, 1992, accessed November 17, 2020, <https://www.ligonier.org/learn/articles/when-doubt-becomes-unbelief>.

78 N. T. Wright, *The Scriptures, the Cross & the Power of God: Reflections for Holy Week* (Louisville, KY: Westminster John Know Press, 2006), 39.

God and His ways are simply too majestic to comprehend, but we can experience His love and grow to understand why He is like He is even if we cannot grasp all the mysteries that surround Him (such as the Trinity). Paul's prayer is appropriate: May we "have power, together with all the saints, to comprehend the length and width and height and depth of the love of Christ, and to *know this love* that surpasses knowledge, that you may be filled with all the fullness of God" (Ephesians 3:18–19; emphasis added).

Once we know the love of Christ, it is much easier to believe in the Bible and its teaching about the cross and the resurrection. Once we truly comprehend all that the grace of God has done, is doing, and will do, everything starts to make sense. Our certainty in God comes from trust, not explanations. We base our hope on what we do not see now, yet we can have assurance of what is to come (Hebrews 11:1). Hope is not wishful thinking or emotion; it is belief that is based on our relationship with God and that He will fulfill His promises. At times, our faith may be more of an "in spite of" than "because of," but our worldview can be well-thought-out and as logical as any other system of viewing the world.

As I have discussed, grace is more than salvation from hell. Much of our journey is experiencing the grace of transformation, a blessing that is appreciated one day at a time. While our faith unto salvation is sufficient for everlasting life, daily faith is a decision that must be worked out. As Dietrich Bonhoeffer related in a confirmation sermon:

> You do not have your faith once and for all. The faith that you will confess today with all your hearts needs to be regained tomorrow and the day after tomorrow, indeed, every day anew. We receive from God only as much faith as we need for the present day. Faith is the *daily* bread that God gives us. You know the story about manna. This is what the children of Israel received daily in the desert. But when they wanted to store it for the next day, it was rotten. This is how it is with all the gifts of God. This is how it is with faith as well. Either we receive it daily anew or it rots. One day is just long enough to preserve the faith. Every morning it is a new struggle to fight through all unbelief, faintheartedness, lack of clarity and confusion, anxiety, and uncertainty, in order to arrive at faith and to wrest it from God. Every morning in your life the same prayer will be necessary. I believe, dear Lord, help my unbelief . . . [for our] Yes to God demands a brave No to everything that will ever hinder [us] from serving God alone, whether it be [our] profession, [our] property, [our] house, [our] honor before the world (emphasis added).[79]

---

79 Dietrich Bonhoeffer, Sermon preached on April 9, 1938, Quoted from *Theological Education Underground: 1937–1940 (Dietrich Bonhoeffer Works)*, ed. Victoria J. Barnett, trans. Victoria J. Barnett, Claudia D. Bergmann, Peter Frick, and Scott A. Moore, Vol. 15 (Minneapolis, MN: Fortress, 2012): 476–480.

Such is the way of the cross which leads to the throne of God.

The grace of God comes to us camouflaged as a demand, for when we allow the Holy Spirit to transform us, we are confronted with an amazing paradox:

> The Christian way is different: harder, and easier. Christ says, "Give me All. I don't want so much of your time and so much of your money and so much of your work: I want You. I have not come to torment your natural self, but to kill it. No half-measures are any good. I don't want to cut off a branch here and a branch there, I want to have the whole tree down. I don't want to drill the tooth, or to crown it, or stop it, but to have it out. Hand over the natural self, all the desires which you think innocent as well as the ones you think wicked—the whole outfit. I will give you a new self instead. In fact, I will give you Myself: my own will shall become yours.[80]

The Christian who desires to hear the words "well done" and perseveres till the end will be transformed into a brave disciple who is not concerned with what others think or what the cost may be. This is where our imitating of other genuine

80 C. S. Lewis, *Mere Christianity* (New York: HarperSanFrancisco, 2001), 196.

Christians is critical. Imitation of them shows us what genuine discipleship is all about. We need to follow Jesus' example as well as Paul's. And we need to follow "the example of other 'Pauls' around us. Discipleship is a process by which we *imitate-as-we-are-transformed*; the process by which we *imitate-in-order-to-be-transformed.*"[81] One such "Paul" came from the most unexpected circumstances.

You Want Me to Do What?!

When I think of the opposition to living for Christ in our times, I default to Mary Magdalene. Despite the marginalization women experienced in Jesus' day, she had the double distinction of being the first human to see Jesus after His resurrection, as well as the first to report the good news of this history-changing event (John 20:1–8). The details supporting Mary's importance are spelled out in Matthew 28:1–10.

Mary was accompanied to the tomb on the first Easter by other women. Before they reached it, a violent earthquake occurred as an angel descended from heaven and rolled back the stone from the tomb. The Roman guard at the tomb was paralyzed with fear. When the women reached the tomb, the angel commanded the women to "not fear." This directive is not an attempt to ignore our emotions in reaction to such supernatural events; they will

81 Michael J. Wilkins, *In His Image: Reflecting Christ in Everyday Life* (Colorado Springs, CO: Navpress, 1997), 50.

surface because that is the way we are wired. We will be afraid of many situations in our walk with Christ. But what this command is saying to us is, "Believe in God and overcome any cowardice that would prevent you from moving forward in your walk with Christ." God had chosen Mary to be the first bearer of the good news of the resurrection, but all this would play out in circumstances that would prove to be threatening to her.

The arguments of skeptics and doubters of the resurrection are prevalent today. In fact, such worldviews remind me of the Roman guards; opposition causes us to be afraid. From personal conversations, as well as social media, those who would believe in a bodily resurrection are faced with ridicule and opposition because of such "unintelligent" and "naïve" convictions. This opposition is in addition to the inward voices that chip away at us, whispering that Jesus was not the Son of God and a resurrected life is only wishful thinking (Romans 6:1–14); or that we cannot really overcome sin and bondage because there is no such thing as a victorious life (1 John 5:4–5); or that Jesus did die on a cross, but He remains dead and buried like anyone else. To deny yourself and follow Jesus consistently is to be open to the unflattering conclusion that you are "to be most pitied" (1 Corinthians 15:19).

But the only faith that survives is the one that is examined, worked on, and worked out, a faith in which one takes God at His Word and seeks to understand everything in light of all the evidence (so Anslem). The angel commanded Mary "to come and see the empty tomb," to sneak past the sleeping solders. As you struggle to believe that Jesus is alive, do so with all your might. We must follow Mary's example to not fear, and then walk right past the enemies that frighten us. Had Mary chosen to give in to her fears, she would have never known what the resurrected life was all about. But she went to the empty tomb and, by her obedience, placed herself in a position to be used by God to reach a lost world. The faith of Mary, no matter if in infancy at this stage, was primed to lead to experiences that would surpass her initial experience at the empty tomb.

Mary positioned herself to meet the living Christ, the One no longer bound by death and ready to welcome all who will accept Him as Savior and Lord. The story of Mary does not end here. She has an important task to do and, in doing it, she meets the living Lord along the way. She is an important example of what dedicated discipleship is all about.

Such discipleship is learned, not inherited, one decision at a time: one bold stand, one defeated temptation, one failure that leads to victory. Mary Magdalene learned to not fear by living a life that was vulnerable to fear. But the amazing thing about Mary was that she was to share the gospel while still learning to not fear. It was not simply a matter of having enough courage to fight through a storm. To overcome your fears occasionally does not necessarily translate into an effective witness. But when your victories contribute to an attitude that will not allow fear to stop you from doing what God desires, when your victories become the rule rather than the exception, you *are learning to not fear*. In other words, she saw the evidence and went to tell others of the good news, and in the process discovered this way of thinking was the new normal: Mary had become the first Easter person. And though there was much learning and overcoming that lay ahead, she was beginning to learn of the power which was now hers: "God's new creation has begun; and you are summoned to be part of that, part of a new world."[82]

Unless we are willing to share what has become real to us, we will never become the Easter person Mary became. Our human nature—even when born again—seeks to find safety and protection from doubt and ridicule. But Mary encourages us to keep moving, for she is obedient and trusting despite circumstances that say otherwise. To "go and tell" others the good news releases power and love in us that even the gates of Hades cannot stop (Matthew 16:18).

Mary's boldness is the quality of being willing to undertake things that involve risk or danger. For her, it surfaced in that she did God's will and continued on the path that He put her on, regardless of the hardship she faced. Her example—to be imitated—reminds us that "Easter is the main event; if you don't believe in the resurrection, you're not a believer" (John Irving). Paul said as much in 1 Corinthians 15. Furthermore, her actions in Matthew 28:1–10 teach us that *we* are Easter people, citi-

---

82 Wright, *The Scriptures, the Cross & the Power of God*, 73.

zens of a new world and a new creation (2 Corinthians 5:17). What God said to her, He says to us: "The scriptures and the power of God are now yours, your strength, your energy, your comfort, your guide because they point to Jesus, the Jesus who died and is alive forevermore and who meets you on Easter morning with greeting and commissioning. Come and see; go and tell; and don't be afraid."[83] This is the essence of discipleship.

83 Wright, *The Scriptures, the Cross & the Power of God*, 73–74.

FIVE

The Audience of One

British Army Major General Charles Gordon (1833–1885) was a brilliant military strategist and commander. He saw action in the Crimean War but became famous for military prowess in his successes in China in the early 1860s. From these victories, he earned the moniker "Chinese Gordon," regularly defeating much larger forces. His devotion to God was equal to—if not more than—his military accomplishments. He was killed (some say martyred) at Khartoum, Sudan, and the accounts and impressions of his death seemingly resulted from his stand for Christ in his life. When it came time for him to die, "he had only a short step home. Like all for whom God's call is decisive, it could be said of him, 'I live before the Audience of One. Before others I have nothing to prove, nothing to gain, nothing to lose.'"[84] "The Audience of One" is God, of course, the One who created us, died for us, and seeks to live with us in all that we do. He calls us to Himself so that we will realize with Augustine that "our heart is restless until it rests in God."

84 Guinness, *The Call*, 74.

Our examination of God's demand of us is energized by His grace for us. He has done so much and promises to walk with us throughout this life. The demand is to motivate us to reach our potential as His children. In the last chapter, we analyzed the overall mindset and worldview of those who follow in discipleship. In anticipation of a close look at how our primary calling plays out in secondary callings, we first need to look at some specific strategies and expectations that will ensure we approach our discipleship well aware of what we can and must do.

We can easily express our dedication to a cause or person, passing that off as commitment. But words spoken—no matter how passionately—fall short of commitment if we do not put our desires into practice. We often refer to Mother Teresa as someone set steady on the straight and narrow, reminding us to "continue to work out your salvation with fear and trembling, for it is God who works in you to will and to act in order to fulfill his good purpose" (Philippians 2:12–13). Commitment is the twin idea of will and deed, for our "salvation is to be understood, not as an objective yet to be reached . . . but as a possession to be explored and enjoyed ever more fully."[85] Our commitment to genuine discipleship is corrupted by our sinful nature (Romans 7:14–20), "but God is effectually and ceaselessly *at work in you, both to will and work*—to recreate our wills and to impart to us his own capacity for effectual working . . . the effectual Worker would make us like himself."[86]

---

85 Motyer, *The Message of Philippians*, 127.

86 Motyer, *The Message of Philippians*, 129.

As discussed in chapter two, God assigns us our *specific* privileges, responsibilities, opportunities, and gifts and empowers us to fulfill these tasks; we must act consistently with courage in completing them. But boldness in specific actions is not something we can turn on and off at will; rather, it is the result of a long-term commitment to a lifestyle that is unappreciated, if not opposed, by secular society. If we fail to take advantage of the chances to serve God, then they will be taken away from those who are not dedicated to Christ and given to those who are (Matthew 25:28–29).

I tip my hat to the boldness of Mary Magdalene, and she should be acknowledged as having lived a superlative life of discipleship. But our thinking on her courage is inadequate if we reduce it simply to the times she performed a fearless act in a time of crisis. Her life—most of which is unknown to us—undoubtedly was one of service, a dedicated disciple. When thinking of boldness and how it relates to Mary, we need look no further than Mother Teresa. When we recount her deeds of mercy, we can easily miss the courage and bravery it took for her to embark on a ministry to the destitute, a ministry which offered little in worldly rewards and was fraught with numerous obstacles, not least of which was the temptation to give up, since eliminating poverty was like David facing Goliath. Her persistence in serving our Lord is boldness in the first degree. She did not quit, and we see her bravery in living out her primary calling. Boldness must grow in us and is not just an occasional occurrence. It is a deep-seated quality that is not learned in a day but matures over a lifetime of discipleship. Obedience is the means to experiencing the grace God offers us, beginning with our initial salvation and continuing throughout this life and beyond. Grace demands obedience; obedience actualizes grace.

We are to do what we have to do (imperative) because we ought to be who we are (indicative), "children of God without fault in a warped and crooked generation" so that we may shine "like stars in the sky" (Philippians 2:15). "*Children of God* describes neither wishful thinking, nor a fond hope, nor a target for supreme endeavor, but a present reality waiting to be worked out in our conscious, responsive behaviour."[87] Those whom God adopted are to be strong and consistent in their discipleship.

What we are addressing here is the disciple who is as daring as a lion: "The wicked flee though no one pursues, but the righteous are as bold as a lion" (Proverbs 28:1). This animal is fearless, attacking other animals greater in size, for their fearlessness is part of their DNA. We can be led to believe that courageous acts of faith will come automatically when, in fact, we must gain deeper knowledge of God in order to claim the boldness which should be ours. It is only through study of His Word, fellowship with other Christians, affirmation of God's will as good, pleasing, and perfect, and obedience that leads to the revelation that in the long run we really do not have to fear anything.

87 Motyer, *The Message of Philippians*, 131.

Furthermore, all of this leads to discovering our true identity in Christ. God did not give us a spirit of fear, but of power, love, and self-discipline (2 Timothy 1:7). In Christ, we are protected (Colossians 3:3).

We remember that fear is not an emotion that comes upon us when threatening situations occur, but rather an attitude that prevents us from living for God as we should. When circumstances present themselves that cause us to fear—criticism at work, ridicule from our family and friends, self-doubt—we usually pray to be removed from or relieved of them. But the lion continues confronting its enemy: "From birth the lion cub instinctively knows to be fearless: it just knows it is a lion . . . The lion cub does not have to pretend to be brave; it just has to be itself." [88] We can do likewise as we come to the truth that God will deal with whatever threatens our walk with Him, remembering that the boldness which God honors and uses is one that is clearly identified by an obedience that is distinctive and visible to all. Such disciples seek to imitate the "lion of Judah" (Revelation 5:5) by being who they are, "the salt of the earth and the light of the world."

Salt and Light

The grace that enables us to pursue holy living results in a life characterized as set apart for God in all our think-

---

88 Martin K. M., "Spiritual Boldness: The Lion in You," Levaire, February 27, 2019, accessed November 24, 2020, <https://levaire.com/spiritual-boldness-the-lionin-you/>.

ing, speaking, and doing. And we progress on two fronts. On the one hand, holiness sets us apart *from* the world. We are the "salt of the earth," the example of purity that reflects a counterculture, a way that rejects the idolatry of modern-day society. Yet hand in hand, we are set apart *for* the world; we are the "light of the world," pointing to our Father who grants us identity in Christ, freedom, and victory, both now and in the world to come. It is impossible to talk intelligently about grace without mentioning the demand that comes with it, and it is impossible to mention demand without acknowledging the grace needed to fulfill it. We cannot discover grace if we do not take its demand seriously, and we will never welcome the demand until we have comprehended what grace has done and will do for us.

A key thought behind this book is to let God have His way in our life, all the time acknowledging that we must cooperate with Him while letting Him "do all the work." By "all the work," I mean He finds us and adopts us into His family, and then proceeds to enable us to consistently seek to live like Him. He transforms our minds and convinces us that He will help us speak and act as He would. Yet He expects us to live our Christ-like lives before others so that they can witness firsthand what God wants to do for them.

This idea of "being in the world but not of the world" is succinctly summarized in the following passage:

> You are the salt of the earth. But if the salt loses its saltiness, how can it be made salty again? It is no longer good for anything,

> except to be thrown out and trampled underfoot. You are the light of the world. A town built on a hill cannot be hidden. Neither do people light a lamp and put it under a bowl. Instead they put it on its stand, and it gives light to everyone in the house. In the same way, let your light shine before others, that they may see your good deeds and glorify your Father in heaven. (Matthew 5:13–16)

Jesus' words on salt and light are part of the Sermon on the Mount (Matthew 5–7), where He teaches His disciples a countercultural, offensive, and disturbing message that will seem foolish yet will result in the only life worth living.

> [The Sermon on the Mount] seems to present the quintessence of the teaching of Jesus. It makes goodness seem attractive. It shames our shabby performance. It engenders dreams of a better world . . . The Sermon on the Mount is probably the best-known part of the teaching of Jesus, though arguably it is the least understood, and certainly it is the least obeyed.[89]

Our passage follows on the heels of the Beatitudes (5:1–12), which conclude with the promise that those who follow Christ will be persecuted, which is no less than a

---

89 John Stott. *The Message of the Sermon on the Mount: The Bible Speaks Today* (Downers Grove: InterVarsity Press, 1978), 9, 15.

reason to rejoice (5:12). The point is as kingdom people, we who live a different life are not going to be appreciated or even tolerated in the world. And yet, our Lord says we will be blessed in ways that are unknown to most. The New Testament does not let us forget that we are salt and light the moment we accept the call to follow Christ. Our orders are to be seen by many and to be different, the privilege and the demand of grace.

We may be tempted to think of salt as simply a commonplace item in Jesus' day, no more important than what you would normally find on a dinner table. But it was an important commodity for the world of Jesus. It could be used as money, seasoning, preservative—all of which show how Christians can be used by God to influence the world for Him. But salt also carried with it the idea of purity (Exodus 30:35; 2 Kings 2:19–22), an element added to sacrifices (Leviticus 2:13), an eternal covenant (Numbers 18:19). Thus, Christians are called to demonstrate holy living, to be instruments to transform the world. We are to be in the world to help it; we are also called to be distinct from the world so that the world will know it is God who offers His help through us.

If we do not fulfill our responsibility, we are rendered useless in the scheme of God's plan to redeem the world. We should not become distracted over the question of whether or not salt can lose its saltiness, for the lesson is clear: Jesus' disciples are "different from the people of this earth, and their presence is necessary as God's means of influencing the world for good."[90] Acting as salt is "proof of the reality" of Christ as Lord of our lives. True disciples will live holy lives; impostors will be revealed for who they are.[91]

Our transformed minds should lead us to speak differently than the world. When was the last time we followed the wisdom of Psalm 19:14, "May the words of my mouth and this meditation of my heart be pleasing in your sight, LORD, my Rock and my Redeemer"? We must consider that our words have a way of revealing what is on our minds and in our hearts. I often fear that the Lord would gladly supply me with a transcript of my words spoken for the day—such an occasion would not always be a time for rejoicing.

Do off-color or vulgar conversations not only not bother us but also originate with us? Paul commands us to "not let any unwholesome talk come out of your mouths, but only what is helpful for building others up according to their needs, that it may benefit those who listen" (Ephesians 4:29). It is so easy to pass along gossip because we think we gain prestige if we share things others do not know. Moreover, if it puts the person who is a thorn in our side in a negative light, then somehow we are seen by others as the better person.

Communicating is a constant activity, whether verbally or electronically. Does our speech share the world's pessimism on so many things? The year 2020 is in the rearview mirror as I type these words—COVID-19, the death of

90 Wilkins, *Matthew*, 213.

91 Wilkins, *Matthew*, 214.

George Floyd and subsequent protesting, the unwelcome negative rhetoric of the presidential election—all of these batter us and weigh on us as we ponder how to respond. Do we find ourselves caught up in emotions of this volatile time? Do comments that shame and vilify us cause us to lose control of what comes out of our mouths or what comes from our fingertips? Do our actions create and intensify tension and division in the form of cliques at church and at work? We need to focus on holy living so as to provide ourselves with a defense and strategy, offering protection against imploding when we let down our guard. If saying whatever comes to mind because everyone else is doing so becomes our default reaction, then living out our primary calling is the furthest thing from our mind, for it is not even an option.

We can improve our environment in general and our discussions in particular by remembering that our conversations must always be "full of grace, seasoned with salt, so that you may know how to answer everyone" (Colossians 4:6). This goes back to our look at the importance of thinking. We should be open to listen to others but whether in a group or one-to-one conversations, we should not let negative and hurtful words pull us away from what we know is pleasing to the Lord. We should direct comments toward what pleases the One who called us and who placed His trust in us. He is the only one in our audience. Our prayer should be that our words be *edifying* of others and *glorifying* to God. It may be needful sometimes simply to walk away from situations where there does not seem a way out without compromising our witness.

Contributing wholesome input to discussions will not always be well received, and sometimes in meetings we just have to sit there and deal with it. If we have thought through our being "set apart" from the world's thinking, then our words will reflect this. We should pray through Scripture for control of our speech. In Psalms 141:3–4 we find this prayer:

> Set a guard over my mouth, Lord; keep watch over the door of my lips. Do not let my heart be drawn to what is evil so that I take part in wicked deeds along with those who are evildoers; do not let me eat their delicacies.

This is where the living out of our faith is clearly accomplished in a foreign environment.

James reminds us: "We all stumble in many ways. If anyone is never at fault in what he says, he is a perfect man, able to control his whole body" (James 3:2). This scripture is not saying perfect in the sense of sinlessness but mature in action by offering sound speech and words that uphold our Lord and bring Him glory.

Another prayer is that we will be "quick to listen, slow to speak and slow to become angry" (1:19). Holy speaking is a learned habit; we are not born with uplifting tongues. The tongue is an unpredictable organ, as James forcefully reminds us:

> The tongue is a small part of the body, but it makes great boasts. Consider what a great forest is set on fire by a small spark. The tongue also is a fire, a world of evil among the parts of the body. It corrupts the whole body, sets the whole course of one's life on fire, and is itself set on fire by hell. (James 3:5–6)

Though the tongue can provide uplifting words, we must also allow the Holy Spirit at times to quiet our tongues because unspoken words that would be hurtful if uttered are also the result of living a holy lifestyle. Such successes are small victories in an ongoing battle.

> Our vocal witnessing is to be gracious and to concentrate on God's offer in Christ, the wisdom of God (1 Corinthians 1:24, 30; 2:6), so that those who hear our words may sense that we are speaking to their need and matching their questionings with God's provision in the message of His love and wisdom in Christ's cross, as in 1 Peter 3:15.[92]

Our gracious talk (or non-talk) can be characterized by discouraging gossip, avoiding slander, and distancing ourselves from off-color stories. We can start to "salt" the world when we use wholesome talk and introduce words of hope. We must know when to remain silent and when to speak

---

92 Ralph P. Martin, *Colossians: The Church's Lord and the Christian's Liberty* (Grand Rapids, MI: Zondervan, 1972), 139.

(Ecclesiastes 3:7b). Both instances are bold, for the former is a display of confidence and patience that all will turn out well, and the latter reaffirms that courage will be rewarded.

At first glance we are tempted to say, "I don't want to rock the boat by imposing my beliefs on those around me, especially in business meetings where I am in the minority as a Christian." But there is a difference between demanding everyone believe as you do and sharing your beliefs. We do not need permission to act like God's holy people, to be God's salt and light. Furthermore, such is both our task and our privilege.

Being "salty" is not limited to what comes out of our mouths. Our actions should also align with our desire to be holy. Holiness is to present God to the world, and to do so in an inviting way. To be set apart for the world is first of all to help make this world *a better place.* We need to offer the love of God to the world, the unconditional love which God has shown us.[93] To be most effective in the world, we must above all else practice such love everywhere—in our home, church, community, and workplace. Such love goes hand in hand with forgiveness: "Be kind and compassionate to one another, forgiving each other, just as in Christ God forgave you" (Ephesians 4:32). Anything close to this approach will stand out in our society in which popular heroes and heroines—portrayed on television and movie screens, as well as in social media—love everyone until they

---

93 This is the agape concept of love that says, "I will seek your highest good no matter what type of person you are to me."

are crossed, and then all bets are off. To exhibit an attitude that doesn't seek revenge will go a long way in showing your holy living, especially if you have been wronged or attacked, or you didn't get the promotion or job you were hoping for, or you are singled out because of your faith.

Closely aligned with love and forgiveness is the attribute of mercy, which moves us to compassion so as to act in difficult circumstances and take on the pain of a community. What about those whose home is destroyed by an affair? Threatened by legal difficulties? Torn apart by misunderstanding and mistrust? You can be a "life-changer" by having a listening ear, even if the behavior of the one you are helping goes against your lifestyle. Or you may be a peacemaker—not in the sense of meddling in everybody's problems, but when two disputing parties both come to you. We can share that we have peace with God (Romans 5:1–2) and the peace of God (Philippians 4:6–7). We can be the avenue of God's peace. We can stand in the gap (Ezekiel 22.30). Holiness says we *stand up and stand out* so that we can offer what the world needs, not stand off and gloat because we think we are better than everyone else, nor stand aside and fail to become involved because we do not want to impose our beliefs. As salt, we bring flavor and purity to our broken world. This is why losing our saltiness is a warning for us: We are called to be holy to help the world. This is what Jesus is commanding, yet inviting, us to do. Make a difference: Be meek and merciful and peace-making and loving to make this world a better place. That is a way to live as one who is saved by grace for grace.

In addition to being salt, we are called to be the light. We know that God is the source of light (Genesis 1:3), His coming is described in terms of light (Isaiah 60:1–3), and God's Word is light (Psalm 119:105). Jesus identifies Himself as the Light (John 8:12; 9:5) who enlightens all people (1:4–14) with the message of salvation (Matthew 4:15–16). Moreover, God's people are called to be the light to the nations (Isaiah 49:6) and to carry the message of Christ to the world (Ephesians 5:8; Philippians 2:15). Yet, like salt that has lost its saltiness, we can hide our light. You cannot hide the light of a city on a hill at night, and why would you light a lamp and place it under a bowl while the room remains dark (Matthew 5:14–15)?

The preceding discussion about being set apart *from* the world can, in a sense, be flipped and examined from the perspective that when we are set apart from the world, we are simultaneously set apart *for* the world. While some of what we show as "salt" encounters pushback in society, at the same time our salt becomes light. Can we approach others expecting nothing in return? Do we help others—even our enemies—by coming with a gracious attitude, doing something for no other reason than we want to share God's grace? Our "set apartness" from the world's actions allows us to be channels of God to touch others.

To be set apart for the world provides help for the world: Our faithful deeds become the light to point to our Father, glorifying Him before the world. In one sense, this is God's gift to us, for He has invited us to share in His seeking a lost world. This layer of grace is our ministry, an opportunity to use our holiness (which is from God) to point the world to the Father. Our being set apart is to lead people to discover why we are salt and light and what or who is our power source. God, in His great wisdom and love, allows us to take His grace to His world. It is a privilege to point others to Him. And what better way than putting shoulder to shoulder to make one's way in this world.

Jesus commanded us to take up our cross, as He took up His. In other words, take God's love to a lost world. Interestingly, outsiders are both curious about why we are different and often resentful at the same time. But we are to live out faith before others—not to impress them, but to point them to God. Our words about the gospel *must accompany* our deeds and our deeds *must reinforce* our words. We should not be on a crusade to win an argument; we need to be respectful and open. Our good deeds and helpful actions should not be simply for humanitarian reasons; they should be performed with the hope of sharing the good news of the gospel and being a channel for inserting the power of God into any situation. When we prove helpful or even successful to the point of special recognition, we should graciously accept the praise. We can thank those who deemed us worthy of acknowledgment, show appreciation to others who supported us in our task, and simply say all we did was to bring glory to God (*soli Deo gloria*).

To be set apart for the world is to live life as Easter people. By this I mean Christians who reveal what it is to live in the new creation of God, as achieved in the bodily resurrection of Christ. The resurrection sets Christianity apart from other religions and belief systems. It's not the thought of a god rising from the dead—that can be found in many other writings besides the Bible.[94] The difference is that believers in Christ have new life in that they will live forever as individuals in the presence of God. Furthermore, they can experience this new life to a certain degree in the here and now, as suggested by the preceding discussions.

Overall, living out our faith is not a list of "thou shalt nots" as much as it is doing what makes us the person God intended us to be. The call to holy living is not simply a light for others, but also our bold adventure for finding a fulfilling life as Christians. To fail to seek to become mature in our holy living will hurt us in the long run. Our desire to be an effective witness for Him will not be accomplished, and we will not experience the full measure of the life God has for us. The primary calling to come to God and to live a life that exhibits that calling is the foundational thought in the Bible. From Abraham until the book of Revelation, the overriding theme is God calling to us to come back to Him and live as His children. We will live out that call in our secondary callings, ever mindful that Jesus' call supersedes anything else in our lives. Such is demanded of a disciple, to live before the Audience of One.

---

94 See descriptions of Osiris, Tammuz, Adonis and Attis, and Dionysus.

When Is a Good Work a 'Good Work'?

Our primary calling to be the salt and light climaxes in Matthew 5:16: "In the same way, let your light shine before others, that they may see your good deeds and glorify your Father in heaven." We find no escape clause for those who might have correct doctrine; we see no way out if we simply want to go along with the crowd. Bonhoeffer reminds us that we are salt and light, and to deny the implications of such designations is tantamount to denying our Lord.[95] Our actions must shine as light before others so that they see the glory of the Father. It is not a salvation earned by works, but a salvation demonstrated by works. Like salt, our actions are to be pure; and our light is to provide direction and insight for a lost world. When practicing these words of our Lord, we show that the kingdom of God is here.

> We bring seasoning and light to the world, not that the world may praise us, but that it may see and fall down before the presence of God in our midst. Salt is lost in the flavoring of food; we do not praise the salt, but the taste of the food. Light is overlooked when it reveals the contents of a room; we do not praise the light, but the items on display. So it is with us: The joy of our calling is to help people discover the glory of God.[96]

---

95 Bonhoeffer, *Cost of Discipleship*, 116–119.

96 John Killinger, *A Devotional Guide to the Gospels* (Waco, TX: Word Books, 1984), 17.

We need to have a good idea of what Jesus is referring to when He mentions the good deeds of the disciples. We can easily limit our understanding to helping those marginalized or in great need. Such actions on the part of dedicated disciples can be ways to direct the conversation to the gospel, especially when the follower of Christ mixes in the good news of Christ with the actions performed. But we must keep in mind Christians do not have a monopoly on good works. Non-Christians can do likewise, so our look here at good works must be expanded, particularly considering the biblical context of Matthew 5:13–16.

Jesus has just announced that persecution awaits those who fulfill their salt and light responsibilities. The words that follow in 5:21–48—not hating, not lusting, turning the other cheek, loving your neighbor—are not the typical actions considered good works as just mentioned. But the essential meaning of good works in 5:16 is that whatever we do can be a means to point to the Father in light of the cross. What our Lord meant is captured by Bonhoeffer:

> Men are not to see the disciples but the good works, says Jesus. And these works are none other than those which the Lord Jesus himself has created in them by calling them to be the light of the world under the shadow of the cross. The good works are poverty, [strangers on a journey], meekness, peaceableness, and finally persecution and rejection. All these

> good works are a bearing of the cross of Jesus Christ. The cross is the strange light which alone illuminates these good works of the disciples. Jesus does not say that men will see God; they will see the good works and glorify God for them. The cross and the works of the cross, the poverty and the renunciation of the blessed in the beatitudes, these are the things which will become visible. Neither the cross, nor their membership in the [church will indicate] any merit of their own—the praise is due to God alone. If the good works were a galaxy of human virtues, we should then have to glorify the disciples, not God. But there is nothing for us to glorify in the disciple who bears the cross, or in the community whose light so shines because it stands visibly on the hill—only the Father which is in heaven can be praised for the "good works." It is by *seeing* the cross and the community beneath it that men come to believe in God. But that is the light of the Resurrection.[97]

While our work in bettering our communities provides a much-needed platform to share the gospel, we must not

---

97 Bonhoeffer, *Cost of Discipleship*, 119.

be caught up in the acclamation we may receive (6:1–4). Rather it is when we love in the name of Jesus, live humble lives, promote and exhibit chastity, and verbally share the good news that we really become the light of the world:

> One's *good deeds,* like a light in the darkness, stand in such bold contrast from one's context that others either recognize and acknowledge the transforming presence of God's role in the disciple's life, or they strongly reject it with the negative consequences of 5:10–12 (cf. Jesus' ministry). Both elements are inherent to Christian ministry, to discipleship. [98]

Simply put, we are bold as lions when "we are fools for Christ" (1 Corinthians 4:10). Either people will glorify God because of our transformed life or consider us to be *a fool, a moron,* one who is weak in understanding or intellect to the point of stupidity. We are fools because we serve a foolish God:

> But God chose the foolish things of the world to shame the wise; God chose the weak things of the world to shame the strong. He chose the lowly and despised things of the world, and the things that

---

98 Robert A. Guelich, *The Sermon on the Mount: A Foundation for Understanding* (Waco, TX: Word Books, 1982), 125.

> are not, to nullify the things that are, so that no one may boast in His presence. (1 Corinthians 1:27–29)

He died on a cross, and He hides Himself from human reason and effort. We will not find God in the great wonders of the universe; we will find Him in the humility, weakness, and suffering love of God as found in the cross of Christ.

We believe in a foolish message, that there is power in the cross. We are saved from the penalty of sin (Ephesians 2:8–9) and will be saved from the presence of sin (Isaiah 35:8–9). But even more ridiculous, we are now being saved from the power of sin (present tense), "For the message of the cross is foolishness to those who are perishing, but to us who are being saved it is the power of God" (1 Corinthians 1:18). And we show this power by living a foolish life: "Then Jesus said to all of them, 'If anyone wants to come after me, he must deny himself and take up his cross daily and follow me. For whoever wants to save his life will lose it, but whoever loses his life for my sake will save it'" (Luke 9:23). Need I say more? Is there anything more absurd to say than "if you want to find true happiness, true freedom, then give up your freedom"?

Living as salt and light before a world that sees strength in getting one's way in the world requires much boldness. But Jesus demands we take up our cross and follow Him. And He explicitly warns us to count the cost if we are going to follow Him in authentic discipleship:

> Which of you, wishing to build a tower, does not first sit down and count the cost to see if he has the resources to complete it? Otherwise, if he lays the foundation and is unable to finish the work, everyone who sees it will ridicule him, saying, "This man could not finish what he started to build." Or what king on his way to war with another king will not first sit down and consider whether he can engage with ten thousand men the one coming against him with twenty thousand? And if he is unable, he will send a delegation while the other king is still far off, to ask for terms of peace. In the same way, any one of you who does not give up everything he has cannot be My disciple. Salt is good, but if the salt loses its savor, with what will it be seasoned? It is fit neither for the soil nor for the manure pile, and it is thrown out. He who has ears to hear, let him hear. (Luke 14:28–35)

All this is to say that sometimes our humanitarian deeds will point to the Father, but also our stand against sin and the culture will direct one's attention to Him; such good works leave us open to persecution and ridicule. This is the spectrum of the meaning of good works. We have all felt the pain of someone turning on a light while we're asleep in a darkened room. Our immediate response is irritation as we pull the cover over our eyes. Such is the response when our actions cast light on the deeds and attitudes of others. We reflect Jesus, who is the Light of the world, into situations where those doing evil deeds do not want their ways exposed (John 3:19–20).

The words of Matthew 5:13–16 describe the essence of discipleship; they were uttered at the beginning of the training of Jesus' disciples, anticipating the day some would hear the blessed confirmation from having done well (25:14–30). So the question becomes how do we even begin to process the commands to be set apart *from* the world and yet set apart *for* the world? In other words, how do we live as though we have only the Audience of One?

Doubling Down

This is a battle since we are continually pressured to conform to worldly standards "yet throughout Scripture the summons is given to a vigorous nonconformity, and warnings are sounded to those who give in to worldliness."[99] This was the warning given to Israel (Leviticus 18:3) and to us (Romans 12:2):

> The constant tendency of God's people was, and still is, to behave "like the heathen," until nothing much seems to distinguish

99 John Stott, *The Contemporary Christian: Applying God's World to Today's World* (Downers Grove, IL: InterVarsity Press, 1992), 25.

> the church from the world, the Christian from the non-Christian, in convictions, values and standards.[100]

We must live holy lives as living before the Audience of One, but this is not easy.

The challenge is to reject the influence of the world while simultaneously taking advantage of our opportunities to impact the world around us. That is, we are called to be holy within the spheres of influence we have, whether at home, at work, or at play. The forces that pull us in different directions will confront us as long as we proclaim that Jesus is Lord of our lives. We must strive to grow in holiness, without which no one will see the Lord (Hebrews 12:14). That is, we must pursue holiness, for this pleases our Lord. Such an endeavor reveals the desire to become more like Christ as well as the depth of our commitment to do so. Although we will never attain the holiness of our Lord, nevertheless our discipleship should be characterized by constant progress in our sanctification. When we were justified and granted initial or positional sanctification, the seeds of progressive sanctification were planted, to be watered by the Holy Spirit as we seek to live out a life that pleases Him.

The counterintuitive lifestyle to be in the world yet never becoming part of the world is the grace and demand of genuine discipleship. Our qualification to be called a disciple of Christ is grace-based, as is living out our disciple-

---

100 Stott, *The Contemporary Christian*, 26.

ship. We recall the twin ideas of indicative and imperative. We have been made right with God; now we must live like we are right with Him. To meet the demand of grace in our lives, we must refuse to forfeit our dual responsibilities of light and salt. We must not hide behind the Word of God so that we fail to confront the world with the light of God's truth. Likewise, we must not imitate the world and thus simply blend in; we must retain our saltiness. John Stott urges us to exhibit a "double refusal," rejecting the two extremes of *escapism* and *conformity*, which "are opposite mistakes, but neither is a Christian option."[101]

Being in the world is clearly a risk. Paul could become all things to all people with the intent of sharing the blessings of the gospel (1 Corinthians 9:19–23) while simultaneously not allowing outside friendships to lead him to deny his faith or make decisions that compromised his beliefs (2 Corinthians 6:14–7:1). On the one hand, "we shall never discover how great and many-sided the gospel is" if we fail to act as light.[102] On the other hand, we will offer no distinctiveness if we conform and simply act as chameleons when we leave our Christian environments to mingle with those who are not Christian.

The Word of God is a means for protection from the influence of the world, but it can only protect us if we are in the fray, fighting the battle before us. The Sword of the Spirit

---

101 Stott, *The Contemporary Christian*, 27.

102 Donald English, *The Message of Mark: The Bible Speaks Today* (Downers Grove, IL: InterVarsity Press, 1991), 85.

is an offensive weapon, meant to help us make our way in all the skirmishes we will face. To light a lamp and place a bowl over it defeats the purpose of our quiet times and Bible studies, for we will not grow in the Lord if we do not follow Him wherever we are. And we will not have the strength or courage to resist conforming to the world if we are not in the Word. We must be bold and go where God can use us; and we must be bold and be His people wherever He places us.

To complement our double refusal, one must practice "double listening."[103] While listening to the Word of God and following its truth, we must also listen to the world—not to accept its ways, but to relate to its hurts and be in position to help it. The disciples of Christ are to "be a light to the nations." We must allow the Word to confront us and allow the Holy Spirit to rebuke us and then to strengthen our walk in holiness. In turn, we must hear the cries of the world and seek to minster to them. Discipleship is all about washing the feet of others, even those who seem determined to oppose us. After all, our Lord washed the feet of Judas of Iscariot on the night He was betrayed (John 13:1–17)! We will be unable to demonstrate the power of the gospel if we distance ourselves from the world (escapism) or become just like the world (conformity); in both cases, the gospel is missing because of us. "Double listening is indispensable to Christian discipleship and Christian mission."[104] And such

---

103 Stott, *The Contemporary Christian*, 27–28.

104 Stott, *The Contemporary Christian*, 29.

action leads us to be relevant and not simply popular, to be significant to God's work and not simply trendy. "We are called neither recklessly to risk ourselves nor timidly to secure ourselves, but to find the point of life-giving tension between the two."[105]

This is difficult in our business or work obligations, where alcohol and possibly risqué behavior threaten our witness and can lead us into compromise. It may be no different in social gatherings. We have to determine our boundaries, so we do not violate our saltiness or place a bowl over our lamps. Jesus dined with sinners and tax collectors (Mark 2:13–17) with the explicit purpose of opening up the door to salvation. Important to holy living is finding our sweet spot, the place where we can comfortably mingle with others who do not share our Christian values and yet, at the same time, not compromise the gospel or our Christian walk. Do our actions and speech match up with our biblical worldview? With those of Jesus? Do they point those around us to God? The disciple dedicated to living for Christ at all times will develop courage and confidence because "living before the Audience of One transforms all of our endeavors."[106]

Day by Day

In the early 1970s, a song titled "Day by Day" was popular. It was based on the prayer of the thirteenth-century English

---

105 English, *The Message of Mark*, 70.

106 Guinness, *The Call*, 71.

bishop Saint Richard of Chichester. The song essentially repeats the words:

Day by day, dear Lord,
Of Thee three things I pray:
To see Thee more clearly,
Love Thee more dearly,
Follow Thee more nearly,
Day by day.

I remember these words partly because they are forever embedded in my mind (!), but mainly because they capture the secret of discipleship: As we faithfully live out our primary calling, we come to see Him more clearly, love Him more dearly, and follow Him more nearly. And we do this day by day.

In the end our discipleship will not be measured by those individual moments when—with the power of the Holy Spirit—we perform commendable acts or resist life-damaging temptations to sin. Instead, for the most part, we will live out our primary calling through the routine and mundane responsibilities of our secondary callings. We will find ourselves taking our children to soccer practice or comforting our spouse who is facing a difficult task; we will worship and serve in churches with others who are struggling with COVID-19 fears or the heartbreak of wayward children or impending divorce; we will find ourselves in the midst of a community divided over race and politics; and we will face the daily pressures of a job that has not brought the fulfillment we expected but instead turned into such a time-devouring calling that we have lost our feel for God. This is discipleship in the twenty-first century.

A natural response to this description of discipleship is that it does not seem as exciting and noticeable as what we find in the four Gospels. But such a reaction fails to comprehend what has been preserved for us. For the most part, we find the twelve disciples/apostles physically following Jesus around for three years. And what these disciples did in the ordinary course of family and community was not deemed significant to include in the Gospels. We know that Peter's (Cephas's) wife accompanied him on some of his missionary journeys (1 Corinthians 5:9) and probably the other members of the Twelve had families too. But such natural activities are left for our imagination. Instead, we read that the Twelve were chosen from a wider group of disciples and designated apostles (Luke 6:13), to be sent out by Jesus on a mission to preach the gospel. They had the *exclusive task* of establishing the Christian faith: "The apostolic band had the unique, unrepeatable position of church-founders."[107] We must keep in mind that while all apostles were disciples, few disciples were apostles. "The term *apostle* has a significantly different meaning than *disciple,* designating as it does the leaders of the early church in Acts. As 'disciples' the Twelve are examples of what Jesus accomplishes in all believers; as 'apostles' the Twelve are specified as the leaders within the new movement to come,

107 Motyer, *The Message of Philippians*, 180.

the church."[108] We can learn much about discipleship from Peter and the other apostles, but we must not allow their unique responsibility to lead us to think that only they and those like them will be entitled to the pronouncement of "well done."

We must live out our faith in Christ just as clearly and earnestly as the Twelve. We must live under the shadow of the cross, knowing that we are sinful people tasked with the awesome responsibilities of being the salt and the light. To embrace a theology of discipleship is to recognize the grace of God and all that He has given to us. In addition to salvation, we have prayer, which "is the door through which God, Creator and Lord, enters into our home, community, and labor."[109] We have His Word at our disposal and of course His Spirit within us. Such means strengthen us to stand firm and be bold in all our tasks. Boldness can teach us perseverance, as we must continue to allow Christ to work through us in all our callings. We are told to love our neighbors as ourselves; and, in doing so, we must not forget our family members are our neighbors just as much as those with whom we come in contact outside our home. Those dedicated to serving others in their secondary callings are those whose discipleship pleases God. "Most people seek God in mystical experiences, spectacular miracles, and

---

108 Michael J. Wilkins, *Following the Master: A Biblical Theology of Discipleship* (Grand Rapids, MI: Zondervan Publishing House, 1992), 113.

109 Gustaf Wingren, *Luther on Vocation* (Eugene, OR: Wipf and Stock Publishers, 1957), 150.

extraordinary acts they have to do. To find Him in [our callings] brings Him, literally, down to earth, makes us see how close He really is to us, and transfigures everyday life."[110]

This last point is made clear in the parable of the sheep and goats (Matthew 25:31–46). In that parable, we are encouraged to see the hidden Christ in all our relationships with God's people. At the last judgment, Jesus separates His people from those who will be lost for eternity; and His standard for acceptance and rejection is not salvation by works but works because of salvation. He rewards the righteous sheep with the inheritance reserved for those who live for Him, and in the process of informing them as to why they are receiving such recompense, He remarks that they had been kind to Him. That is, they have ministered to Him by sharing food and drink, and reaching out to those in loneliness, poverty, sickness, and imprisonment (25:35–36). The sheep express surprise at this statement, only to be informed, "Whatever you did for one of the least of these brothers of mine, you did for me" (25:37–40). We serve Christ wherever we are, whether our service is known to many or just a few. We perform for our Audience of One, no matter the number of people observing our actions.

---

110 Wingren, *Luther on Vocation*, 24.

SIX

Charity Begins at Home

When Rev. Paul Gibson retired as principal of Ridley College at Cambridge, a painting of him was unveiled. He offered an astute comment when asked his thoughts on the portrait. He said, "In the future, people looking at the picture would not ask, 'Who is that man?' but rather, 'Who painted that portrait?'"[111] Our prayer should be, "May people not praise us but the One who painted us."

I begin our look at discipleship in the home with this simple illustration because, of all the secondary callings, this is the most critical. Yet the irony is that we may focus less on this calling than the other three—especially our vocation. If others of our household can remark about us as Rev. Gibson proposed—even though they see us daily—then truly we have taken discipleship in the home quite seriously. For this is where we are seen on those days we didn't get much sleep, are worried about paying the mortgage, are

111 John Stott, *The Message of Ephesians: The Bible Speaks Today* (Downers Grove: InterVarsity Press, 1979), 82.

trying to find time to perform the routine tasks of cutting the grass and making lunches, face the challenging years of teenagers, enforce curfews, address bad grades, and wonder why a child's room continues to look like a disaster area. This is where our discipleship is to be lived most intentionally, and this is where our "well done" is most crucial and yet most elusive.

We are to be the handiwork of God in the home, an example of what His grace can do. The picture of ourselves "hanging" on the walls of our homes is the one that most truly captures who we are, for those closest to us see this portrait daily. We must realize that if we can't love and cherish those who share our tables and our beds, we will not be effective at church, in the community, and in the workplace.

Home Is Where the Heart Is Revealed

But even more is the beauty, "For we are God's workmanship, created in Christ Jesus to do good works, which God prepared in advance as our way of life" (Ephesians 2:10). In painting our portrait, God recreated us to do good works. While the mention of good (*kalos*) works in Matthew 5:16 emphasizes the kind of actions that direct people to the life of discipleship, here the concept of good (*agathos*) works highlights the practicality of our activities.[112] God has prepared specific work for all of us to do, to live out our

112 William Barclay, *New Testament Words* (Philadelphia, PA: The Westminster Press, 1974), 151–161.

primary calling in the different areas God has planned to use us. We must keep in mind that our call to discipleship is to live it out in everyday life. A vast majority who will read this book will not find themselves on the mission field or behind the pulpit. Rather, they will find themselves behind the wheel driving family members to appointments on short notice or behind a desk trying to meet quotas and deadlines.

This is where we live for our Lord, and this is what He planned for us before the creation of the world. In our secondary callings of home, church, community, and vocation, we fulfill our primary calling to discipleship and must maximize opportunities to achieve the success of a disciple that will hear the words, "Well done!" Our discipleship is conducted in our callings, and we must utilize what grace has provided us to adapt to what it demands in our particular settings.

> We know what God wants us to do; God has prepared long beforehand the kind of life He wants us to live and has told us about it in his Book and through his Son. We cannot earn God's love; but we can and must show how grateful we are for it, by seeking with our whole heart to live the kind of life which will bring joy to God's heart.[113]

---

113 William Barclay, *Letters to the Galatians and Ephesians: The Daily Bible Study* (Philadelphia, PA: The Westminster Press, 1976), 105.

God knew who would be a part of our lives when He gifted us and trusted us to be His hands, His mouth, and His heart wherever we are. And what better place for us to realize such service than in our home.

Except for the calling of serving a church, non-Christians have homes, take part in community service, and work in their vocational areas. Though they may speak of their calling, there is, in fact, no calling if there is no Caller. But we have a Caller, One who "sees and addresses us as individuals—as unique, exceptional, precious, significant and free to respond."[114]

> [Serving God in our secondary callings] is largely a matter of finding where God is, the God who hides Himself in our neighbors, in ourselves, and in the world. Once we notice the Hidden God and realize how He is at work—in our workplace, families, the community, and the church—and when we realize the part we play in His design, we have [realized] our [primary calling].[115]

Perhaps Martin Luther (1483–1546) has it right when he remarks that even washing diapers can be enhanced when done for the glory of God: "God, with all his angels and

---

114 Guinness, *The Call*, 24.

115 Veith, *God at Work*, 60.

creatures, is smiling, not because that father is washing diapers, but because he is doing so in Christian faith."[116]

Our Home

The basic secondary calling is the home, as it can provide the foundational teaching of God and model the way of dedicated discipleship in order to reap the full benefit of grace. At the same time, the home is the most private calling, out of the public eye; our work at the church, our service in the community, our input and output in the workplace are open to the scrutiny of many. But what we do and how we conduct ourselves behind closed doors is off limits to most people. The task of the man and the woman united in marriage is to live as salt and light which, in turn, prepares children to do likewise. Parents are to be a bridge to God, not a stumbling block (Ephesians 6:4).

The institution of marriage is vital to a stable and solid home. The first home was created by God. With the creation of Eve, God established the first marriage with the blessed words, "For this reason a man will leave his father and his mother and be united to his wife, and they will become one flesh" (Genesis 2:24). Scriptures picture God's relationship with His people in terms of a marriage: "For your Maker is your husband—the LORD Almighty is

---

116 John Zehren, "Martin Luther. The Estate of Marriage, 1522" (Translated by Walther I. Brandt), accessed December 1, 2020, <https://www.1215.org/lawnotes/misc/marriage/martin-luther-estate-of-marriage.pdf>.

his name—the Holy One of Israel is your Redeemer; he is called the God of all the earth" (Isaiah 54:5). The church is the bride of Christ (Revelation 21:2, 9) as we see marriage opening and closing the Bible. The value of marriage is further enhanced by Paul's thought that the relationship between Christ and the church provides the divine ideal of what a marriage should look like:

> "For this reason a man will leave his father and mother and be united to his wife, and the two will become one flesh." This is a profound mystery—but I am talking about Christ and the church. However, each one of you also must love his wife as he loves himself, and the wife must respect her husband. (Ephesians 5:31–33)

For Paul, it is not that a strong marriage provides insight into the relationship between Christ and His church, but the other way around; the intimacy of Christ and His bride reveals the depth of intimacy that a marriage can attain. This is seen especially in the idea of "becoming one flesh." The physical act of sexual intercourse is sanctioned by God as part of the marriage relationship, so that the man and woman find a union not only between their bodies but also their personalities, emotions, and spirits. Here we see an example of the many freedoms of marriage and yet the boundaries which are meant to protect it. The sexual relationship is encouraged by Paul (1 Corinthians 7:3–5) yet clearly to be honored and protected by faithfulness to one's spouse (Hebrews 13:4). The Bible teaches:

> God designed marriage as a lifelong commitment between one man and one woman for their mutual joy, the good of society, and the procreation of children. Marriage ultimately displays the glory and grace of God by picturing the unbreakable relationship between Christ and his church.[117]

When the family functions as God intended, it "can be a parable of the kingdom of God," representing the new covenant between Christ and His church.[118] The oneness of Christ and the church is what the Christian couple should strive for because "the Lordship of Christ and His relation to the church epitomize the ideal union between husband and wife."[119]

The husband and wife are disciples sent out two by two. They are to encourage, support, and challenge each other, but most important they are to love each other as themselves. Women and men are equal in God's sight (Galatians 3:28),

---

117 "Marriage to the Glory of God" *Desiring God*, accessed November 27, 2020, <https://www.desiringgod.org/topics/marriage>.

118 Francis W. Beare, *The Interpreter's Bible. Vol. X* (Nashville, TN: Abingdon Press, 1953), 727.

119 Arthur G. Patzia, *Ephesians, Colossians, Philemon: New International Biblical Commentary* (Peabody, MA: Hendrickson Publishers, 1990), 267.

though they differ in their responsibilities in the marriage relationship. They both bear God's image (Genesis 1:26–27), all the while complementing each other. They are to submit to each other in their own way (Ephesians 5:21). Furthermore:

> Wives, submit yourselves to your own husbands as you do to the Lord. For the husband is the head of the wife as Christ is the head of the church, his body, of which he is the Savior. Now as the church submits to Christ, so also wives should submit to their husbands in everything. Husbands, love your wives, just as Christ loved the church and gave himself up for her to make her holy, cleansing her by the washing with water through the word, and to present her to himself as a radiant church, without stain or wrinkle or any other blemish, but holy and blameless. In this same way, husbands ought to love their wives as their own bodies. He who loves his wife loves himself. After all, no one ever hated their own body, but they feed and care for their body, just as Christ does the church—for we are members of his body. "For this reason, a man will leave his father and mother and be united to his wife, and the two will become one flesh." This is a profound mystery—but I am talking about Christ and the church. However,

> each one of you also must love his wife as he loves himself, and the wife must respect her husband. (Ephesians 5:22–33)

The love Paul envisions is sacrificial:

> The love he has in mind for the husband sacrifices and serves with a view to enabling his wife to become what God intends her to be. So the "submission" and "respect" he asks of the wife express her response to his love and her desire that he too will become what God intends him to be in his "leadership."[120]

The headship of the husband has been a source of controversy, a function that has been abused and challenged in the twenty-first century. But such observations do not negate the responsibility of the husband. Marriage should be an exchange of wisdom of both partners, as both serve each other in their respective roles:

> Instead, whoever wants to become great among you must be your servant, and whoever wants to be first must be your slave—just as the Son of Man did not come to be served, but to serve, and to give His life as a ransom for many. (Matthew 20:26–28)

120 Stott, *The Message of Ephesians*, 231.

The husband and wife are to walk side by side in fulfilling the purpose of the home. This is why Paul directs married couples to look to Christ and His relationship with His bride when processing the different roles in a marriage. While in a Nazi prison and unable to attend his niece's wedding, Dietrich Bonhoeffer wrote a wedding sermon; in it, he remarked, "It is not your love that sustains the marriage, but from now on, the marriage sustains your love."[121] The home is the means that sets the tone for discipleship in our other callings.

The boldness to become "one" is a salt and light statement. When the couple teaches and upholds the sanctity of marriage, practicing sexual faithfulness and upholding the commitment needed to fulfill the wedding vows, the two who have become one are progressing in their sanctification. Sex is clearly sanctioned, but only in a marriage of a man and a woman. The partners are to fulfill each other sexually, and sex is never to be used to punish or dominate; it is a blessing from God (1 Corinthians 7:3–5).

Their love for each other is a solid basis for the love for their children. A task contained in the calling of the home is that the man and woman instill in their children what discipleship is all about: "Start children off on the way they should go, and even when they are old they will not turn from it" (Proverbs 22:6). Part of the treasures God

---

121 Richard Schwedes, "Lutheran Weddings," October 4, 2007, accessed December 1, 2020, <https://lutheranweddings.blogspot.com/2007/10/weddingsermon-by-dietrich-bonhoeffer.html>.

gives us at conversion is our responsibility to be a parent. If anything, having children drives home the concept of unconditional love, meaning we love them before we even conceive them, and nothing will stop us loving them. That does not mean they will not reject such love and break our hearts, for this possible outcome is included in the secondary calling of establishing a home. But we must strive to be faithful in our responsibilities as parents, for we must teach our children the ways of God: "Talk about [God's commandments] when you sit at home and when you walk along the road, when you lie down and when you get up" (Deuteronomy 6:7).

A major challenge of building a home is the many roles that come with it. We are spouses and parents and may still be children ourselves. Also, we are siblings and in-laws, creating the situation where we serve different functions for different people. What often happens is role conflict, for as I take time to help my parents, in the process I may have to reschedule time with my children. And when you add our roles in the church, the community, and the workspace, there is never a time we make everybody happy. Yet it is in all our roles in our secondary callings that we must live out our discipleship. A faithful follower of Christ must be just as diligent in the home as elsewhere. We do not want to be faithful in our other callings only to fail to be so in our home.

This is not to expect perfection, but to acknowledge that we are sinners; that is why there is the need for grace.

We will sin *in* our callings, for we are guilty of impatience, lack of concern, selfishness, and falsehood. We fight to reject the idols of success, status, and materialism. We may have to combat the evils of addiction—such as pornography, alcohol, drugs, and gambling—as well as the trials of miscarriages, broken dreams, and desired vocations that remain out of our reach.

Above all else, we must not sin *against* our callings by pushing God out of our lives and pushing away those who mean the most to us. Many of us have heard the example of placing a frog in a pan of water on the stove. By increasing the temperature of the water just one degree per hour, the frog ultimately is boiled to death—unawares! If we have made the biblical worldview our own, then we should not let our guard down just because we can be "ourselves" at home. One way to measure our progress in sanctification is how we treat people, no matter the context. We should always treat people well, starting at home. If we are unkind to those who live under the same roof, then likely we will treat others in the same manner. Furthermore, if we are easy to get along with in society while exhibiting ill-mannered conduct towards others at home, then this situation is unhealthy and hypocritical to say the least. Neither bodes well for one who is seeking to follow Christ as salt and light. Love does not harm its neighbor. "Love must be sincere. Detest what is evil; cling to what is good. Be devoted to one another in brotherly love. Outdo yourselves in honoring one another . . . Love does no wrong to its neighbor. Therefore love is the fulfillment of the law" (Romans 12:9–10; 13:10). And our family members are our closest neighbors!

Words such as love, grace, forgiveness, and repentance should permeate our relationships with our family members. Our walk in public should mirror the dynamics of a home dedicated to God. Issues of doubt, sexuality, morality, racism, and politics will eventually hit home. And our ability to listen and converse as a family is a good training ground for how we will act in the outside world. In our homes, we will not escape the need to demonstrate the good works as described in Matthew 5:16, including actions that will receive pushback as we refrain from attending events or supporting popular causes that send the wrong message about our convictions. These matters will arise with our children and other family members, and we need to be open to listen; sometimes the Holy Spirit will advise us to be quiet and let the other person vent. Often dialogues that begin with a respectful give-and-take approach devolve into point-counterpoint arguments. The fear of such outcomes does not excuse us from addressing difficult topics, but we should be aware of how division can result from what seemed like a good process at the time. We should be "innocent as doves and wise as serpents" when confronted with worldviews that oppose our Christian faith.

I taught a course on Christian ethics in college. One of the main emphases was the development of one's ethics and how *to relate* to those who hold different understandings. The point I attempted to make is that when we envision a strategy on how to respond to those who view morality differently than us, we do so with a family member in mind. My hope was that if students would do that, they would be more empathetic with the other people and desire to understand them instead of rejecting them out of hand. It's easy to condemn and stereotype those with whom we may never have contact; it is quite different when dealing with those who live under the same roof. If one could be prepared to dialogue instead of attack, then such an approach would impart peace to the home and provide a plan for dealing with such matters in the world.

Our home can provide the greatest opportunities to show that Christ is a real and transforming presence in our lives, and, at the same time, it can be the source of our greatest heartbreaks and disappointments. To love your spouse as promised at your wedding speaks volumes of the power of Christ. To be patient and understanding, yet firm, with your children goes a long way in teaching them who their true Father is. The home provides the greatest venue to discover the symbiotic relationship between grace and demand. We recall that knowledge is essentially useless until it becomes action. Obedience leads to deeper intimacy with Christ. When we realize what union with Christ can mean for us, we make the great discovery. We experience the reality of the resurrection in taking up the cross and fulfilling our roles in the family.

We know all too well the situations and temptations that threaten a discipleship-like home. We cannot eliminate all attacks of life that threaten our home, but we can develop a strategy to stand our ground. Showing thankfulness to God for all the blessings and coming together as a couple to support one another during dark times as well as times of stress will provide a coping mechanism to survive and grow as a family. Paul's words of wisdom are relevant for the happiness of a home:

> Do not be anxious about anything, but in every situation, by prayer and petition, with thanksgiving, present your requests to God. And the peace of God, which transcends all understanding, will guard your hearts and your minds in Christ Jesus. Finally, brothers and sisters, whatever is true, whatever is noble, whatever is right, whatever is pure, whatever is lovely, whatever is admirable—if anything is excellent or praiseworthy—think about such things. Whatever you have learned or received or heard from me, or seen in me—put it into practice. And the God of peace will be with you. (Philippians 4:6–9)

We have peace with God (Romans 5:1–2) because of our salvation, but we need the peace of God to head off the flaming arrows that damage or even destroy a home. Peace from God is a trust that no matter our circumstances—whether facing trials such as COVID-19, financial challenges, relationships that are fragile, or even death—God will take care of us. Our faith in God dispels fear and conquers the evil one, leaving us to grow no matter what life brings.

Paul shares with the Philippians that he had learned the secret of contentment (4:11–13). He had progressed in his faith to the point that he was able to accept that he needed few things in this world. This understanding was not so much the result of a decisive and memorable event as it was a slow but determined process of discipline. He developed an attitude that was dependent on God alone for peace and contentment and not on things he possessed or trouble-free times. He could face all things because Christ gave him strength. Two times Paul says that *he learned* that nothing could touch him.

We can have faith that peace *with* God is abiding and will not fluctuate, as will the peace *from* God. Unpaid bills, job insecurity, demands outside the home, illness, jealousies, disobedient children, moral failures—all this and more can rip the peace of God from our hearts if we are not careful. The idea of peace includes the qualities of wholeness and completeness as contained in the Jewish concept of *shalom*, something Jesus wants for His disciples (John 14:27). Our Lord desires that we experience the Father, but this presence must be invited in with trust and love. We must work to put ourselves in place to receive this presence, this peace. We are to pray for peace from God because "the way to peace is in prayer to entrust ourselves and all whom we hold dear to the loving hands of God"[122] To do so places a guard against losing our way, both in terms of a crisis as well as those tough stretches that make us want to give up. To help keep anxiety and other torments out of our thinking, we are to think on the things of God, for His peace "passes" or "transcends" our understanding. It is a component of the fruit of the Spirit (Galatians 5:22) and is a supernatural reality, not as the world gives. "The Lord is my rock, my fortress, and my deliverer; my God is my rock, in whom I take refuge, my shield and the horn of my salvation, my stronghold" (Psalm 18:3).

All this is to say that husbands and wives are to emulate what the life of dedicated discipleship is all about. When a wife experiences the love of a man who wishes to love her as Christ loves the church, she will learn the depth of God's love *for* her. When a man senses his wife respects his leadership, he will be empowered to live for Christ in a deeper manner. And when children witness these two people—committed to God and each other—they will have reason to build their love on the way of God because it works in their home. There may be times the parents struggle with what has hit them, but those who learn contentment—no matter the times of trial and error—will show that one can cope and live lives characterized by peace and joy; we pass on the spiritual lessons needed for life by our actions. May

---

122 William Barclay, *The Letters to the Philippians, Colossians, and Thessalonians: The Daily Bible Study* (Philadelphia: Westminster Press, 1975), 78.

our words and deeds in the midst of trial and tribulation demonstrate that our heavenly Father grants us peace and victory in the severest of circumstances. I cannot emphasize enough how our discipleship in the home not only enhances our to dedication to Christ but speaks volumes to those with whom we have contact.

Developing a solid Christian basis for a home will always be a work in progress. We mature as we obey and receive new revelation. We will develop a *modus operandi* as a family unit for coming together to face difficult times. Trust must be felt between family members, so that they feel free to share fears, anger, and hurts, all the while knowing that all conversation done in love has the potential of leading the members of the home to a closer fellowship with each other and the Lord. For Christians, home is where discipleship begins, no matter how uneven and chaotic life may become. Discipleship will often seem like periods of trial and error, of learning about what it means to live in Christ, so that "we grasp the new creation which he has made possible, and the entirely new life which results from it."[123] This quote accurately describes our need for holy discipleship in the home.

In our hectic times, the training of children becomes an ongoing challenge. Family time will become precious and "teaching moments" may have to be utilized on the run sometimes. But this doesn't mean parents are off the hook or that all is lost. Ancient advice is helpful here:

---

123 Motyer, *The Message of Philippians*, 180.

> Hear, O Israel: The LORD our God, the LORD is one. Love the LORD your God with all your heart and with all your soul and with all your strength. These commandments that I give you today are to be on your hearts. Impress them on your children. Talk about them when you sit at home and when you walk along the road, when you lie down and when you get up. Tie them as symbols on your hands and bind them on your foreheads. Write them on the doorframes of your houses and on your gates. (Deuteronomy 6:4–9)

A few suggestions are always saying grace (in public as well as home), family devotions, discussing Sunday School or youth meeting lessons, and pointing out God in His creation. Explaining why "trending" activities or movies are helpful or not in our walk with God is another way to train our children.

As children grow older, the influence of the parents may seem to diminish. This is why discipline is vital and must always be exercised. However, the older a child becomes the harder it is, and the challenge becomes how to gain obedience instead of simply demanding it and expecting it. This is where love and understanding, perseverance and grace, salt and light come to the forefront. Not all children respond to the gospel and even if they do, when they become teenagers and older, they may not see that their discipleship includes honoring their parents. This heartbreak may continue long after they have moved out of the house. Yet investing in the lives of children continues throughout the parents' life, even when the responsibility of loving our children unconditionally can be painful and heartbreaking; but such is the duty and calling of parenthood. This is where the parents need to support—not blame—each other in such difficult circumstances. This is why joint discipleship in the home is essential.

Discussion in this chapter so far assumes that both spouses are believers. Such couples are not spared difficult circumstances, such as just discussed. But if either spouse is not a Christian, then a new layer of challenges comes into play. If one of the marriage partners is not a believer, it is impossible to achieve the intimacy God desires for married couples. This will become painfully apparent when difficult times arise and long-term situations develop. What you have is different spouses looking to different sources for strength and healing. This is why marrying an unbeliever is to be discouraged and avoided. Paul discusses what to do when one partner becomes a Christian *after* the marriage. He shares that if both parties agree for the believer to pursue his or her faith, then realistically peace may be attained to a certain degree; and if such an agreement is maintained, then the home should remain intact. Our apostle keeps open this possibility. But as a realist, he is open to the alternative that peace may not be prevail and separation or even divorce is the viable option (1 Corinthians 7:12–16).

Quite challenging is the home devastated by death or divorce. The loss of a parent through death can easily send a family into a tailspin, and the emotional and spiritual pain may take years to heal, if ever. Furthermore, the feeling of rejection and betrayal by the spouse that is left behind in a divorce places an undue burden on them as they try to remain civil in bitterly contested custody battles, especially when communicating to the children how to move on. Sometimes the call to discipleship is very painful when our home seems on the brink of destruction. Nevertheless, those single parents who refrained from tossing away their faith and stick it out with their children will rightly be heroes and heroines in their eyes. Sometimes the unexpected appearance of God in the storms of life has resulted in remarriages that hold the potential of what we have mentioned above.

In mentioning the home, the number of persons is not the determining factor in establishing a solid base for Christianity. Such homes may have only one member in the household. Not to be overlooked are those Christians living a life of celibacy. Paul considers such a state as a gift, using the same term (*charisma,* 1 Corinthians 7:7) as he does when referring to the gifts of the Spirit (12:4). Paul is not against marriage; one does no wrong to marry, but he thinks it is better to remain single (7:38). John Stott, celibate his entire life, remarks, "The gift of singleness is more a vocation than an empowerment, although to be sure God is faithful in supporting those he calls."[124] He felt that though the single life must include a certain degree of loneliness and the need for self-control in terms of sexual energy, such challenges could be "redirected both into affectionate rela-

124 Albert Y. Hsu, *Singles at the Crossroads: A Fresh Perspective on Christian Singleness* (Downers Grove, Illinois: InterVarsity Press, 1997), 178.

tionships with friends of both sexes and into loving service of others," so that those whose secondary calling of the home includes singleness "can find joyful self-fulfillment in the self-giving service of God and other people."[125]

Those who are single are often the designated "aunt" or "uncle" to nieces and nephews. This can provide a unique ministry that those in a household of several cannot accomplish. However, those with other family members in their home must not assume singles have any more time than anyone else. They too have activities and other secondary callings to live out.

The secondary calling of the home deserves attention because it is foundational to one's discipleship. Solid homes are essential for a strong local church, as well as establishing a Christian presence in world. We must not fail to give the home its due, as we can easily focus on discipleship everywhere else. On the other hand, a strong showing of discipleship in the family is not enough. We have other callings in which to be the salt and light of the gospel. The home is the place where we first establish our discipleship and often the context where we finish our walk with the Lord; perhaps we should say that our discipleship begins and ends in the home.

---

125 Stott, *The Message of 1 & 2 Thessalonians,* 84–85.

SEVEN

Let the Party Begin

New Testament scholar N. T. Wright shares a humorous incident he experienced while riding in a taxi in London. In small conversation, the driver asked Wright what he did for a living, and he answered he was a Bishop of the Church of England. A few more words were exchanged when the driver said something quite unexpected. "The way I look at it," he said, "is this: If God raised Jesus Christ from the dead, all the rest is basically rock 'n' roll." Immediately Wright texted a colleague, sharing what he had just heard. The colleague texted back that Wright had his Easter sermon, which is now online.

What did the taxi driver mean? Since Christ has been raised from the dead, then the task and privilege for us is to let the good times roll. For those who take salvation seriously, then rock 'n' roll naturally follows in our discipleship. Wright notes that the music is played in the key of new creation, "that though we get it badly wrong, when we face up and say 'Sorry' God forgives us because of the cross of Jesus Christ and shows us how to live out the implications of that costly forgiveness; that though death, corruption and deceit appear to have the last word, God raised Jesus Christ from the dead."[126] This is what it is all about, and we as a church are to invite the world to join our party. This party will be inviting if and only if we in the church support each other and walk hand in hand over all of life's hills and through all of life's valleys.

Our Church

Just as we are called to our human family, we are called to our spiritual family, manifested in the local church. The local church represents the entire church (the universal church):

> It is not part of the church but is *the church* in its local expression. This means that the whole power of Christ is available to every local congregation, that each congregation functions in its community as the universal church functions in the world as a whole, and that the local congregation is no isolated group but stands in a state of solidarity with the church as a whole.[127]

126 N. T. Wright, "Resurrection and Rock 'n' Roll," April 4, 2010, accessed December 4, 2020, <https://ntwrightpage.com/2016/03/30/resurrection-androcknroll>.

127 Ladd, *A Theology of the New Testament,* 537.

We become a part of this community so that we might worship our Lord with other believers, observe the ordinances of baptism and communion, learn about God's Word for our lives and discipleship, be strengthened by other believers, and in turn use our spiritual gifts along with our natural abilities to build up the body of Christ "until we all reach unity in the faith and in the knowledge of the Son of God, as we mature to the full measure of the stature of Christ" (Ephesians 4:13).

Above all else, the church we join should be a body of believers that supports our idea of discipleship. This is important, as members need to strengthen and encourage each other in their walk with God through their walk with one another. The term behind church is *ekklēsia*, meaning "called out ones." The idea of God's people in community reaches back to the Old Testament. When Stephen was speaking before the Sanhedrin in Acts 7:38, he referred to Moses as belonging to the congregation (ESV; *ekklēsia*) in the wilderness. God initiated the practice of calling His people *out* of the sinful world and into His holy community. It was His plan to reach the world through His "called out ones," His saints, the salt and the light. Peter paints the picture exquisitely for us:

> But you are a chosen people, a royal priesthood, a holy nation, God's special possession, that you may declare the praises of him who called you out of darkness into his wonderful light. Once you were not

> a people, but now you are the people of God; once you had not received mercy, but now you have received mercy. Dear friends, I urge you, as foreigners and exiles, to abstain from sinful desires, which wage war against your soul. (1 Peter 2:9–11)

Those who have accepted Christ as Savior and Lord are to draw sustenance from other Christians:

> And let us consider how we may spur one another on toward love and good deeds, not giving up meeting together, as some are in the habit of doing, but encouraging one another—and all the more as you see the Day approaching. (Hebrews 10:24–25)

We need each other to walk in faithful discipleship. Therefore, it is of the utmost importance to join a congregation that is clearly committed to the foundational beliefs that have been mentioned throughout this book. The clear path to salvation in Christ and what it all means should be front and center for the church's beliefs. The need for God's grace in reconciling and sanctifying us must be demonstrated in the preaching, teaching, and discipleship training. The importance of the Word of God and the part it plays in conveying the primary calling of God through the gospel is a good litmus test as to how your dedicated discipleship will be received and supported in your church. God's grace as experienced in fellowship with the Holy Spirit continues to work in us through the Word from the day of our salvation until we see Him face-to-face (1 Thessalonians 2:13); the importance of the local church in this journey is incalculable.

Before visiting a congregation for the first time, it is wise to obtain all the information you can through visiting a website. This way, you can ascertain the church's beliefs and positions on issues that interest you. A visit to a worship service and new members' class will help inform your decision to join or not. If the church you are considering does not hold dear to what the Bible clearly teaches, then you need to move on. I am not implying there is a perfect church with perfect people out there somewhere. We are all sinners in need of grace and sanctification. Every church will have its weakness and its strengths, and we will contribute to both categories. We will not all think alike in our Scripture interpretations. But key areas of agreement are these: (1) our God is Three Persons in One; (2) the authority of the Bible; (3) the only path to salvation is the death and resurrection of Jesus Christ, the Divine Son of God; (4) we are all called to be the salt and light by sharing and living the gospel in a dark world; and (5) someday Jesus is coming again to establish God's kingdom on earth once and for all.

The pastor's demeanor will also contribute to our overall understanding. He is to live out his discipleship in his vocational calling and should demonstrate a clear understanding and a right handling of the Word of God (2 Timothy 2:15). He is to preach a sermon based on Scripture, true to the Word and applicable to the twenty-first century. All teachings and decisions are based on the Word, and he works with the boards that oversee the work of the church. He delegates the work of the kingdom to those who are seeking to live a life of faithful discipleship. He works with those who share their gifts, training them and leading them in areas such as teaching, discipling, visiting the sick, and ministering to those in need. In the process, he must protect the church from false teachings: "He must hold firmly to the trustworthy message as it was taught, so that by sound teaching he will be able to encourage others and refute those who contradict this message" (Titus 1:9). We must pray for and respect the pastor and be willing to assist him any way we can. As laypeople, we can assist the pastor as we have more access to places that are unreachable to him. The pastor faces a daunting task, and while we cannot ignore questionable behavior and deviation from the time-honored truths of Christianity, we must support him all we can.[128] After all, if the apostle Peter could not walk on water, then why do we expect our pastor to?!

The church will have different people with different needs, which should lead me to ask myself if my discipleship at the church contributes to unity. By unity, I mean

---

128 Dr. Jim Meyer, "Churches that permit verbal assaults on their pastor sow the seeds of their own destruction," Restoring Kingdom Builders (blog), accessed January 1, 2021, <https://blog.restoringkingdombuilders.org/tag/complaining-about-a-pastor/>.

is Jesus Christ proclaimed as Lord and those of His body nurtured by what I do? Do my actions promote oneness among other members so that Christ is in our midst (Matthew 18:20) and we hear His voice (John 10:27)? We must heed Paul's words on unity within diversity.

> Just as a body, though one, has many parts, but all its many parts form one body, so it is with Christ. For we were all baptized by one Spirit so as to form one body—whether Jews or Gentiles, slave or free—and we were all given the one Spirit to drink. Even so the body is not made up of one part but of many. Now if the foot should say, "Because I am not a hand, I do not belong to the body," it would not for that reason stop being part of the body. And if the ear should say, "Because I am not an eye, I do not belong to the body," it would not for that reason stop being part of the body. If the whole body were an eye, where would the sense of hearing be? If the whole body were an ear, where would the sense of smell be? But in fact God has placed the parts in the body, every one of them, just as he wanted them to be. If they were all one part, where would the body be? As it is, there are many parts, but one body. (1 Corinthians 12:12–20)

Regardless of gender or social status or ethnicity, we are to be one body. That does not mean that we all think alike or look alike, for we will be diverse (Revelation 7:9). But the passage teaches that our Lord's body is organically related. We are to use our gifts and responsibilities to strengthen the body. Our distinctions should not prevent us from unity in Christ; rather, when we become one, we bring our varied resources and thus honor the Lord by showing ourselves and the world that, though different, we are of one accord.

The local church must be a place where we and others can exercise our *talents*. Perhaps we can teach a Sunday school class or participate in a small group, where we develop deep relationships with other believers. Maybe serving on boards or committees will be an avenue to share what treasure God has given us. We can use our natural abilities to serve in community outreach. Part of our discipleship is accepting the task given to us. We must not go for a power grab because of our ego or allow jealousy and envy to lead to resentment of others in the spotlight. Furthermore, we must be aware of how the family members in our home fit into the church.

As a means of grace, our spiritual gifts exhibit themselves for the outworking of our discipleship, particularly in our church. In addition to the gift of the Spirit Himself, God has given special gifts to all Christians, by which we serve other Christians for the common good (1 Corinthians 12:7). Such gifts, while residing in individuals, are really manifestations of the Spirit.

Paul has provided us with four main lists of the gifts (*charismata*):

1 Corinthians 12:8–10	**1 Corinthians 12:28–30**	**Ephesians 4:11**	**Romans 12:6–8**
Wisdom	Apostles	Apostle	Prophecy
Knowledge	Prophets	Prophet	Serving
Faith	Teachers	Evangelist	Teaching
Healings	Miracles	Pastor	Exhortation
Miracles	Healings	Teacher	Giving
Prophecy	Helps		Leadership
Discernment	Administration		Mercy
Tongues	Tongues		
Interpretation	Interpretation		

A quick glance at this table reminds us that some gifts are more visible—more noteworthy in terms of prestige—than others. But they all are to be used for the purpose of building up others in their walk with God. Our gifts are to demonstrate that the Holy Spirit rules our lives and that we are servants of one another:

> Each of you should use whatever gift you have received to serve others, as faithful stewards of God's grace in its various forms. If anyone speaks, they should do so as one who speaks the very words of God. If anyone serves, they should do so with the strength God provides, so that in all things God may be praised through Jesus Christ. To him be the glory and the power for ever and ever. Amen. (1 Peter 4:10–11)

Our spiritual gifts are a further reminder that God's grace is meant to be an endless resource for our growth as we live a praiseworthy life as a disciple of Christ. "We are called to use our gifts in service within the church to build up the body of Christ, to strengthen the body, and to carry out its purpose within the world."[129]

We must remember that other church members are also fulfilling their secondary calling in the church. Unity does not require uniformity on everything, but you cannot have unity without allegiance to Christ and His Word. Otherwise, we sacrifice unity for a place where half-truths can be encouraged in order to simply get along with each other and the world. The words of Gene Edward Veith Jr. are helpful here:

> Christians should join together in worship with those whose faith and theology they share. The members of a congregation need to be unified. If a church body embraces many different theologies and practices, there will be lack of unity. It is far better, in my opinion, to have a diversity of churches than to have a diversity of theological positions within a single church, a condition that can only lead to vagueness, inconsistency, and confusion of teaching. But how can any one tradition claim to have the whole truth? Well,

129 Whelchel, *How Then Should We Work?*, 76.

> believing in something means to believe that it is true. Each Christian should be in the church that he or she thinks has, as close as possible, the whole truth—that is, the best understanding of Scripture. The church is to be both unified and diverse.[130]

A latent opponent of unity is the pettiness and pride that lurks in our hearts, both of which contribute to our feeling of superiority. The second letter of C. S. Lewis's *The Screwtape Letters* is a clear indictment of our petty-mindedness. We think we have a superior religiosity when compared to that of those who "sing out of tune, or have boots that squeak, or double chins, or odd clothes." Such unconscious or denied mean-mindedness on our part stifles our taking the other person seriously as a brother or sister in Christ. Likewise, the ego-feeding feelings that come with holding a special office or responsibility in our local church or denomination prevents us from seeing the truth that we need other Christians to grow in Christ as we should. Paul is quick to remind us of this truth:

> For by the grace given me I say to every one of you: Do not think of yourself more highly than you ought, but rather think of yourself with sober judgment, in accordance with the faith God has distributed to each of you. (Romans 12:3)

---

130 Veith, *God at Work*, 128.

At times, we may hold certain positions or elected offices in our church that bring us accolades and recognition. More likely, we often find ourselves working one-on-one with people who need encouragement or support in their walk. Maybe their households are struggling or their work is becoming unmanageable. Perhaps a particular sin has come to dominate their lives. Is God asking of us to commit the time and energy to work with our fellow Christian? Are there programs and strategies in place to help? Or both?

The church is central to God's purpose for communicating the gospel. It is to be the light of the world, yet it will be ineffective if it loses its saltiness (distinctiveness). We are called to fellowship with other Christians—that is, to participate in each other's lives through the work of the Holy Spirit. Such fellowship enables God's people to present a dynamic alternative to a lost and hopeless world. The effectiveness of the New Testament church was based on the solidarity of believers as they interacted with each other in the power of the Holy Spirit. "They devoted themselves to the apostles' teaching and to fellowship, to the breaking of bread and to prayer" (Acts 2:42). Paul's appeal to the Ephesians for unity is a worthy goal for your church:

> As a prisoner in the Lord, then, I urge you to live a life worthy of the calling you have received. Be completely humble and gentle; be patient, bearing with one another in love. Make every effort to

> keep the unity of the Spirit through the bond of peace. There is one body and one Spirit, just as you were called to one hope when you were called; one Lord, one faith, one baptism; one God and Father of all, who is over all and through all and in all. (Ephesians 4:1–6)

Our apostle knew firsthand that we will never reach our potential as disciples nor experience the intimacy with God which can be ours if we fail to take advantage of genuine fellowship with fellow believers. Our interaction and conversations should be meaningful, intentionally focusing on one's walk with God and not limited to merely socializing with other brothers and sisters. What seems apparent is that without an emphasis on such fellowship (*koinonia*), a local church will not reach its potential because its members will not reach theirs!

But God's resources do not end here; in fact, they can increase exponentially when we think of what the Spirit provides for us, including His fruit. One of many blessings awaiting those who come to God for salvation, accept His Son the Savior, and allow the Spirit to set up permanent residence in the heart is that of the fruit of the Spirit:

> But the fruit of the Spirit *is* love, joy, peace, forbearance, kindness, goodness, faithfulness, gentleness, and self-control. Against such things there is no law. (Galatians 5:22–23; emphasis added)

It is interesting to note that the term fruit is singular not plural. We do not have "fruits of the Spirit" but "fruit of the Spirit," composed of nine godly characteristics. The significance of the singular is that if you want to truly possess one of the different characteristics of fruit, you must possess them all.[131] Furthermore, this is another example of how our discipleship must be intentional, that is the fruit of the Spirit "is *both* the gift of God *and* the result of the person of faith making conscious decisions to cultivate this way of life and these habits of heart and mind."[132]

This is reinforced by Paul's recognition that only the disciples who have crucified the flesh can keep in step with the Spirit (5:24–25). To "walk in line" with the Spirit is to say with Paul, "I have been crucified with Christ and I no longer live, but Christ lives in me. The life I now live in the body, I live by faith in the Son of God, who loved me and gave himself for me" (2:20; see 6:14). This reference to crucifixion plainly shows the difficult nature of progressive sanctification: "Crucifixion does not lead to a quick or easy death; it is an execution of lingering pain. Yet it is decisive; there is no possibility of escaping from it."[133]

The path to transformation is hard and long, yet it is the only way to allow grace to produce the desired results. As we seek to live holy lives, *we become God's grace to other believers*. The fruit will permeate our lives as we repudiate

---

131 Wright, *After You Believe,* 195.

132 Wright, *After You Believe,* 197.

133 Stott, *The Contemporary Christian,* 155.

sin and self, surrendering to our Lord day by day. The fruit is an act of grace, a source for living as our Lord did and being refashioned into the image of God. We do not wander into a fruitful life simply because we are Christian; we must make it our intention to progress in holiness. We have great potential to serve our brothers and sisters with such fruit, but it is no secret that we can stifle the growth of other Christians by our misuse or even lack of use of what the Spirit has invested in us. Fruit is not automatically apparent and effectual in a Christian's life. To ensure that the fruit will grow and mature in our lives requires that we fight to prepare our hearts and minds to be fertile ground for its growth.

It is no mistake that the first characteristic of Paul's list is love, the most important component to him (1 Corinthians 13:13). If we are to utilize the fruit of the Spirit, we cannot do so if we fail to love. It has been called *the preeminent Christian grace,*[134] for by it we can love God with all of our being, as well as our neighbor. Paul models love for other Christians. When writing to the Philippians, he shares his deep love for them: "Therefore, my brothers and sisters, you whom I love and long for, my joy and crown, stand firm in the Lord in this way, dear friends" (4:1). "We have a long way to go before we are feeling the emotions of Christ towards each other as Paul was—we who so easily dismiss from our reckoning those whom God has accepted and reconciled, and who so lightly offend those for whom Christ died" (see

---

134 Stott, *The Contemporary Christian*, 146.

1:8; Romans 14:3, 15–20).[135] Our love for fellow sisters and brothers in Christ goes a long way in showing who we are (John 13:34–35). And a lack of love is apparent when there is division in the church:

> I plead with Euodia and I plead with Syntyche to be of the same mind in the Lord. Yes, and I ask you, my true companion, help these women since they have contended at my side in the cause of the gospel, along with Clement and the rest of my co-workers, whose names are in the book of life. (Philippians 4:2–3)

Paul was well aware of how the lack of unity—for whatever reason—cripples the effectiveness of a church and its members. He believed:

> Only a united church can hope to face its foes and stand firm. Where there is disharmony inside, there is bound to be defeat outside. Where Christians cannot bear the sight of each other, they will not be able to look the world in the face either. They cannot win on the "main front" of their contact with the world if they are secretly carrying on warfare on a "second front" of their own devising.[136]

---

135 Motyer, *The Message of Philippians*, 200–201.

136 Motyer, *The Message of Philippians*, 203.

It is no accident that Paul concludes his list of characteristics of the fruit of the Spirit with self-control or self-restraint. Just as strategically placed explosives can bring down buildings, lack of self-mastery can demolish any effectiveness of the fruit in a Christian's life. Our living out the grace and demand of God's new life calls for us to contribute what we can to build a unified body. Otherwise, we disqualify ourselves from the opportunity to have run our race well, of having fulfilled a discipleship worthy of the words "well done."

In the preceding chapter we saw how the fruit of peace can impact one's home for Christ. Here we must note that joy must describe the church, for joy is the conviction that because of Jesus Christ's death and resurrection, we are kingdom people who find fulfillment in obeying the Father's—the King's—demand. Something new has happened—namely, the kingdom of God has entered history, and we are part of it. We ask in the Lord's prayer that the kingdom come in its fullness, that "God's will be done on earth as it is in heaven" (Matthew 6:10). But we are to be joyful because this kingdom has already come, God's reign as King commenced with Christ's life, death, resurrection, and the outpouring of the Holy Spirit. As God reigns in our life the kingdom is here, His rule is a dynamic reality while we await the full disclosure of His power. The kingdom is here, for on occasion, we see "what it looks like when God is in charge."[137]

---

137 N. T. Wright, *Simply Jesus: A New Vision of Who He Was, What He Did, and Why He Matters* (New York, NY: HarperOne, 2011), 82.

You Didn't Answer the Question

The new creation has begun, and the church, the body of Christ, is called to be salt and to be light. We are promised a victorious life, one that overcomes the world (1 John 5:5). Fulfilling our calling in the church may find us standing arm-in-arm with fellow Christians and resisting the pluralistic and crowd-pleasing stances of society that essentially support the age-old philosophy of "everyone should do what is right in their own eyes" (Judges 21:25). At other times, we will be working side by side with those of the faith as we move out into the community to serve. At times, such outreach will be easy as we join in community projects and movements to help the poor and marginalized. But in today's world, another kind of outreach beckons us to serve with utmost urgency. And that is dealing with living in the age of the pandemic, which attacks not only our bodies but our souls as well.

It is incumbent upon the church to step up and provide leadership in a world gone mad. How do we answer those—within the church and without—who ask why an all-loving, all-powerful, and all-good God allows the COVID-19 pandemic? No doubt this is a question we have asked ourselves and been asked by others. But I am afraid that in attempting to answer this question we as Christians have developed a self-induced paralysis. We should not avoid such discussions, but these are really academic in nature. And while they may provide a basis for enlightening and challenging dialogue, they offer little that can be applied to personal pain when COVID-19 (or the like) strikes near and dear to one's heart. The anxiety and pain that accompany sickness and death are never lessened by worldviews that can provide intellectual rationale as to why there is evil but offer no hope to deal with it when it happens.

We sometimes put undue pressure on ourselves to defend God (and ourselves!) against the inexplicable tension of why God allows suffering and evil.[138] This leads to feelings of marginalization and lack of relevancy for a world racked with COVID-19. If not careful, we can fail as churches to perform one of our main functions in society: being instruments of God to alleviate suffering.

Our discipleship demands we become vulnerable by admitting we do not always understand God's way, but we can experience peace in all that happens. We possess the hope that all will be okay:

> Fear has become so pathologically present that it is no longer even recognized; it has come to be so part of the air we breathe that we do not even know it is there . . . [And] secular society has no capacity to look truthfully and critically at the source of this paralyzing fear.[139]

Life will never be the same, where even going to the grocery store threatens our well-being; this is the new normal.

---

138 Such a defense is called a theodicy.

139 Gordon T. Smith, "Preacher, Do Not Be Afraid," featured in Matt Woodley's *Preaching Today* Newsletter, December 21, 2020.

Instead of asking why, we should ask and answer the question, "What?" What should we do to aid and comfort those impacted by this virus (or other crises)?[140] Nothing is wrong with considering the first question: Is the crisis due to a "good world that has gone wrong"?[141] Is God judging the world? What complicates matters is that we need to recognize there is a place for philosophical discussions, but they do little if anything when suffering is on the personal level.

We fumble our responsibility by asking the wrong question. The question of what to do is answered in Matthew 25:31–46. Our joy is found in helping people because we have hope that God is working to bring about something new in the world today, even if the answers to why certain things happen escape us. We are not called to play God but to represent Him in all we do. Our task is to love people; God's task is to change them. We often recall Romans 8:28 ("And we know that God works all things together for the good of those who love Him, who are called according to His purpose") and rightfully so. But we must not let these words come from our lips without understanding the full implication.

This verse is in the context of Paul describing deep prayer, so deep words are inadequate to express what God is doing:

---

140 N. T. Wright, *God and the Pandemic: A Christian Reflection on the Coronavirus and Its Aftermath* (Minneapolis, MN: Zondervan, 2020), 3.

141 Lewis, *Mere Christianity*, 42.

> In the same way, the Spirit helps us in our weakness. We do not know what we ought to pray for, but the Spirit himself intercedes for us through wordless *groans*. And he who searches our hearts knows the mind of the Spirit, because the Spirit intercedes for God's people in accordance with the will of God. (Romans 8:26–27; emphasis added)

We recognize the groanings of our world and groan for others as we groan for ourselves, for we perceive a gap between what we are as frail and suffering children of God and what we will be someday in the consummated kingdom of God—namely, gloriously resurrected children of God. Not surprisingly, we do not know now how to pray; graciously, however, the Spirit prays in our stead and amazingly does not use words but instead communicates through sighs and groans. Not knowing how to pray is not something "to be ashamed of. It is a natural place to be" for the calling of the church is "*to be in prayer, perhaps wordless prayer, at the point where the world is in pain.*"[142] Our presence and our loving actions are what the world needs.

Romans 8:28 is not a call to a Christian version of Stoicism, a call to simply tough it out and eventually all things will work themselves out. Rather, it contains the thought that God Himself co-operates for good *with* those

---

142 Wright, *God and the Pandemic*, 44–45.

who love God, for Paul is showing us the suffering and redeeming providence of God.

> God's people are themselves not simply spectators, not simply beneficiaries, but active participants. They are "called according to his purpose," since God is even now using their groaning, at the heart of the world's pain, as the vehicle of the Spirit's own work, holding that sorrow before the Father, creating a context for the multiple works of healing and hope. Such God-lovers are therefore shaped according to the pattern of the Son: the cruciform pattern in which God's justice and mercy, his faithfulness to the covenant and to creation, are displayed before the world in tears and toil, lament and labour.[143]

We are not beholden to provide rational answers to everyone who struggles with the problem of evil. We gain insight into this issue when we look at Luke 13:1–5:

> Now there were some present at that time who told Jesus about the Galileans whose blood Pilate had mixed with their sacrifices. Jesus answered, "Do you think that these Galileans were worse sinners than all

143 Wright, *God and the Pandemic*, 51.

> the other Galileans because they suffered this way? I tell you, no! But unless you repent, you too will all perish. Or those eighteen who died when the tower in Siloam fell on them—do you think they were more guilty than all the others living in Jerusalem? I tell you, no! But unless you repent, you too will all perish."

Jesus is not teaching how to decipher the causes of evil, whether human or natural. Rather, He is saying that death can come unexpectedly to one whether they are righteous or not. And when we hear of such tragedies we are to immediately reflect on Jesus' death for our sin and how short our time is. Hopefully, such introspection will motivate us to reach out to others with mercy, both in our actions and our words of hope. The world needs our compassion more than our philosophical insights.

Among other things, our calling to the church is to develop confidence in the sovereignty of God (God is in control). Such a solid foundation is imperative for a discipleship that is worthy of commendation.

> [God's sovereignty] provides a vital answer to the question which lies behind a lot of speculation and argument about how to apply the Bible to great and disturbing events of our own time. The New Testament insists that we put Jesus at the centre of the

> picture and work outwards from there . . . The point is this. *If you want to know what it means to talk about God being "in charge of the world," or being "in control," or being "sovereign," then Jesus himself instructs you to rethink the notion of "kingdom," "control" and "sovereignty" themselves, around his death on the cross.*[144]

Jesus' life and death are God's way of demonstrating that He is in control—that His kingdom is here, and this is what it looks like when He is in charge. And He shows the world He is in control through people (that is, through us) who follow their Lord's model and look to the cross as the ultimate hope for life. Such a worldview leaves unanswered why suffering and pain is the context in which God exercises His control. Yet God's sovereignty comes through to others who see us living and hoping in God even in our fear and grief. Helmut Thielicke puts it well: "Faith will always be a venture . . . it will involve not a Because but a Nevertheless."[145]

Now, grief and loss should not be the only times we feel the world needs to hear the gospel. We should always be on the lookout for open doors to share the good news; shame on me if I think about being the light of the world only when a pandemic strikes, that somehow in dire times

---

144 Wright, *God and the Pandemic*, 19, 25.

145 Helmut Thielicke, *Modern Faith and Thought* (Grand Rapids, MI: Eerdmans, 1990), 563.

I will face less resistance because people need hope like never before. Those outside of Christ live lives that have no permanent purpose or meaning, or are riddled with addiction and betrayal, or have reached the point of hopelessness; this is what the cross is about. Christ defeated the powers of Satan on the cross (Colossians 2:15), bringing peace to all of creation (1:20) though presently we joyously await our Savior's return and the removal of suffering and pain from the new creation (Revelation 21:4).

When tragedy or difficulty strikes, we as the body of Christ must ask who needs our help, how we can supply this need, and who is best gifted to do so. Money may be available to get someone through a difficult span, or we may offer services and labor to help. Sometimes, we can offer only ourselves. Often, I can only utter the prayer of "strength for today and hope for tomorrow," and then offer myself to help usher in the day that the loss will not hurt so much.

> The good news of Jesus can look truthfully and powerfully *and hopefully* at the source of our paralyzing fear because we know the One who told us, "Do not be afraid." He has come. He is here. He has died for our sins and risen to give us new life. He will restore all things and wipe away every tear. He is the Source of the peace that conquers our fears and anxieties.[146]

---

146 Woodley, "Preacher, Do Not Be Afraid."

In other words, our Lord says, "It will be okay."

When called upon to deliver a funeral message, I share that we often feel like Mary the sister of Lazarus, who fell at the feet of Jesus and accused Him of not caring enough to prevent the death of her brother (John 11:28–35). Jesus did not respond with any justification of her loss; rather, He simply wept. Maybe the greater miracle when Lazarus was raised was not his resuscitation but that Christ "stooped to identify himself without reserve with our condition, mingling his tears with those of Mary."[147] We are not primarily called to provide any rationalizations for evil and suffering, which—in the long run—will never ease anyone's pain anyway; we are called to weep along with the grieving person and minister to them. I am reminded of a telling remark of Dorothy Sayers: "What do we find God 'doing about' this business of sin and evil? . . . God did not abolish the fact of evil; He transformed it. He did not stop the Crucifixion; He rose from the dead."[148] We must not be fearful of wading in the lives of those facing the pandemic simply because we do not have an airtight explanation for difficult situations. Our calling to the church is to weep with those in the church and without.

Church is where we remind (and are reminded by) our brothers and sisters that the cross points to the second

---

147 Motyer, *The Message of Philippians*, 90.

148 Dorothy L. Sayers, "The Greatest Drama Ever Staged," June 1938, accessed December 7, 2020, <http://www.gutenberg.ca/ebooks/sayers-greatest/sayers-greatest-00-h.html>.

coming, the full expression of the kingdom of God. This energizes our desire to meet the demands of grace. Those of us who love Jesus and His cross and His second coming look forward to the day we finally take full possession of the total salvation gained when we accepted the work of the cross. We are citizens of heaven as we await our Lord's return (Philippians 3:20) and "while we wait here, we must live as if we were there."[149]

The calling of the home is foundational for our other secondary callings; the calling of our church complements them. The first two should feed off each other and become a beachhead for our work in the community and our vocations. But we must not take the calling to the church as anything less than an intentional venue to serve our Lord. May the joy of the Spirit produce the hope that shows we know who holds our future, and if so, let us get on with the party. Such is the calling of the disciples who please their Master.

---

149 Motyer, *The Message of Philippians*, 198.

EIGHT

Not of This World

The nephew of William Kelly (1821–1906), preacher and Bible scholar, took a course in the classics at the university and was asked by his professor how he had come to translate Greek passages so beautifully and with such accuracy. The young man shared that his uncle had helped him. The professor requested a meeting with the uncle and that was arranged.

When they met, the professor shared how impressed he was with the skill of Kelly and inquired as to his vocation. Kelly replied, "I am a preacher and travel here and there all over the country ministering the Word of God to groups of Christians." Quite surprised at this answer, the professor harshly replied, "Man, you're a fool." Immediately came Kelly's reply, "In whose eyes, professor?"[150]

Simply put, we serve a foolish God (1 Corinthians 1:20–25), believe a foolish message (1:18), and live a foolish life (Galatians 6:14). In short, we are fools for God

150 Fool Sermon Illustrations, accessed December 10, 2020, <http://www.moreillustrations.com/Illustrations/fool.html>.

(1 Corinthians 4:10). In Paul's day, the term *fool* (*mōrōs*) meant one who is weak in understanding or intellect, to the point of stupidity. When push comes to shove, the community we live in will often side with the Greek professor and consider our commitment and worldview to be foolish, to be moronic. Our *community* is the place we live with other people outside our home and church. We live together in an ordered way, making decisions about how to do things and sharing the work that needs to be done. As disciples, we are to glorify God as citizens in good standing, serving "God's purposes in the world through civic, social, political, domestic, and ecclesiastical roles."[151] As Puritan author William Perkins describes it, there is "a certain kind of life ordained and imposed on man by God for the common good."[152] But as our secondary calling of living in community unfolds and is determined by our obedience to our primary calling, we often can find ourselves out of sync with those with whom we interact every day.

Beware of Sightseers

During his second missionary trip, the apostle Paul found himself in Athens, Greece. Paul's time in this city known for great learning provides a good picture of what we encounter today in our community. Like today, com-

151 Whelchel, *How Then Should We Work?*, 76.

152 William C. Placher, ed., *Callings: Twenty Centuries of Christian Wisdom on Vocations* (Grand Rapids, MI: Eerdmans, 2005), 262.

munity life in Paul's day involved much diversity as well as prejudice. There was the Greek and the Jew, the privileged and the marginalized, male and female, and the nonreligious and religious—both the monotheist and polytheist. I have found that the lessons gleaned from Paul's visit to Athens (Acts 17:15–34) offer a paradigm for living out our discipleship in a secular society.

When Paul arrives in Athens, he apparently takes in the sights and sounds of this great city. But soon he ceases to be a tourist and becomes a critic, greatly distressed at the presence of numerous idols (17:16). He reflects God's provocation and anger at idolatry, such as when Israel built the golden calf (Exodus 32). Paul was one who had "the passion of a man who found in Athens capacity for God, and that capacity degraded and spoiled for lack of God."[153] This is not unlike our society today, where our idols act as a substitute for God:

> Any person or thing that occupies the place God should occupy is an idol. Covetousness is idolatry (Ephesians 5:5). Ideologies can be idolatries. So can fame, wealth and power, sex, food, alcohol and other drugs, parents, spouse, children and friends, work, recreation, television and possessions, even church, religion and Christian service.[154]

---

153 G. Campbell Morgan, *The Acts of the Apostles* (Grand Rapids, MI: Fleming H. Revell Company, 1924), 412.

154 John Stott, *The Message of Acts: The Bible Speaks Today* (Downers Grove: InterVarsity Press, 1990), 291.

And to make matters worse, such idolatry is not discouraged, for much described in the quote is considered normal and promoted as the "successful life" in the twenty-first century.

Despite Paul's indignation, he does not leave Athens in protest or travel around the city with a loudspeaker promoting the virtues of Christianity like one selling OxiClean. He settles in and visits the synagogues, where he can share his thinking with those who resist idolatry. We also find him in the marketplace (*agora*) daily, reasoning with the people there and no doubt sharing thoughts and asking questions (Acts 17:17). For us, the marketplace is our neighborhood, our eating establishments, soccer games, and town or city council meetings. Added to these is the idea of the "public square," a term which has become a metaphor for the occasions when people share ideas and implications in (hopefully civil) discourse, both face-to-face and on social media.

During Paul's time in the marketplace, he encountered Epicurean and Stoic philosophers; some accused him of being a "babbler," a person who plagiarizes the thoughts of other teachers and passes them off as their own. Others assumed his message about Jesus and the resurrection referred to two foreign gods. In the end, they took him to the council of the Areopagus, the High Court of Athens, where the philosophers could examine his new teaching in a private setting (17:18–21). Of note are the worldviews represented by the two groups. The Epicureans were at best practical atheists, either not believing in any gods or considering them so remote they had nothing to offer for their lives. They sought a life of peace and pleasure, an escape from things that caused them pain. This is the picture of our secular society of today. Their counterparts, the Stoics, believed as pantheists do, that God was somehow within people and in nature. They believed that the world was governed by Reason (*logos*; see John 1:1, 14) and the life one lived was determined by fate. Humans must learn to accept what happens in their lives, becoming self-sufficient by developing a stoic, even a fatalistic, response to events.

Paul's point of departure when sharing his thoughts with the philosophers was not a "cut to the chase" message about salvation. Instead, he was led by what God had laid on his heart; the Athenians were consumed by superstition and idolatry and thus blinded to who God is. Paul knew the dangers of idolatry as evidenced in his letter to the Romans:

> For although they knew God, they neither glorified him as God nor gave thanks to him, but their thinking became futile and their foolish hearts were darkened. Although they claimed to be wise, they became fools and exchanged the glory of the immortal God for images made to look like a mortal human being and birds and animals and reptiles. Therefore God gave them over in the sinful desires of their

> hearts to sexual impurity for the degrading of their bodies with one another. They exchanged the truth about God for a lie, and worshiped and served created things rather than the Creator—who is forever praised. Amen. (Romans 1:21–25)

Though the statues and images around Athens were works of art, they had become representations of what people considered most important. They personified what the people worshipped, what the Athenians deemed as worthy of total allegiance. Yet in confronting this vexation, Paul sought to win the person over to the gospel rather than win an argument. Our apostle "complimented" the philosophers on their religious posture, even the erecting of an altar to the Unknown God (Acts 17:22–23). In no way did Paul agree with them, but he disarmed them—for the moment—by pointing out that they were seeking the God Paul already knew.

Paul recognized that some of the philosophers sensed there was something or someone "out there." This thought points to *general revelation,* a term referring to the belief that God as Creator of the universe has placed in the hearts of humans the awareness that He exists and is powerful (17:24–27; see Romans 1:19–20). Revelation is the *self*-disclosure of God, and the qualifier "general" is applied because the knowledge is general or indirect, and available to all. However, general revelation is inadequate for salvation; it is understood to be a situation where we know about someone but do not know them personally. Thankfully, the Bible teaches there is more to revelation.

In addition to general revelation is God's *special revelation*, the specific unveiling of our sinful predicament and the grace of God as found in the cross and resurrection. The source for learning such great truths is the Bible, from which we can discover that we can enter into a personal relationship with God. Special revelation marked His relationship with Israel in the Old Testament and reached its climax in the Incarnation, the personal visit of the Father to earth in the person of His Son. When one hears and responds to the gospel, the Holy Spirit becomes a deeper source for understanding the mind of God.

Paul quotes some Greek thinkers and poets (17:28), thus reminding us that general revelation may flicker in non-Christian thinking, though "special revelation must control and correct whatever general revelation seems to disclose."[155] The apostle is thinking in similar terms as the nonbeliever while building toward the presentation of the truth of the gospel. He had developed the strategy to become "all things to all people so that by all possible means some might be saved" (1 Corinthians 9:22).

Paul continues with the thought of God as the Creator and the Sovereign Lord, able to work out His purpose (Acts 17:24, 26). He presents the truth that God is close, and the altar to an Unknown God is their way of reaching out to Him (17:27), for He does not depend on us but we

155 Stott, *The Message of Acts*, 285.

on Him (17:25). Furthermore, such a Deity is not limited to images or idols or simply abstract propositions; rather, He is transcendent and not restricted to human consciousness and nature (against the Stoics); yet at the same time, He is personal and able to be found by those who seek Him (against the Epicureans). We receive the good news along with the bad: The coming of Christ secured the reconciliation of humanity to God but also pointed to the set day of judgment (17:31). All must repent or face condemnation. Paul's balanced presentation included the idea of a day of reckoning, for we should not simply try to entice those we witness to by omitting the truth of the cost for rejecting grace.

Note that our apostle emphasizes that the reason we know that a day of reckoning is coming is that God raised the man (Jesus) from the dead. We find no mention of the destruction of Athens in 86 BC at the hands of Rome as a reason to repent, as though such a fate may be in the making again if they do not repent. Paul is not into the blame game because he wants to move forward. As Jesus predicted, wars and natural disasters—famines, earthquakes, and plagues—will happen and yet the world is not ending (Matthew 24:6–8). Catastrophes are not so much an eye-for-an-eye payment from God as a signpost that all the evil in this world should point us to the cross. All must repent.

What progress Paul was making during this meeting is unclear. But what is clear is that when he referred to the resurrection, the meeting ended abruptly; some of the philosophers scorned his message, considering him foolish; others politely invited him back. Luke, the author of Acts, summarizes Paul's stay in Athens by reporting that a few men believed the gospel, including Dionysius, a member of the council. Also, a woman named Damaris came to faith, though it is unlikely she would have been part of the Council; probably she heard Paul's message when he visited either a synagogue or the marketplace (Acts 17:34).

Our Community

From our brief look at Paul's experience in Athens, we can identify four principles for living out our faith in our community. First, we must follow the lead of the Holy Spirit when He places us in those situations that potentially rob our Lord of the glory due Him. He is Lord and someday will be honored by all:

> Therefore God exalted him to the highest place and gave him the name above all names, that at the name of Jesus every knee should bow, in heaven and on earth and under the earth, and every tongue acknowledge that Jesus Christ is Lord, to the glory of God the Father. (Philippians 2:9–11)

Paul treasured the Great Commission (Matthew 28:19–20) and loved the Athenians, but Paul's "highest incentive of all is zeal or jealousy for the glory of Christ . . . Whenever he is denied his rightful place in people's lives, therefore, we should feel inwardly wounded, and jealous for his name."[156] This world is His, and our discipleship should be energized by the words of Abraham Kuyper: "There is not a square inch in the whole domain of our human existence over which Christ, who is sovereign over all, does not cry: 'Mine!'" When we are in situations that reject and degrade the glory of God, we must allow the Holy Spirit to calm and lead us so that we can be instruments used of God. In our unique way, God will work through us to restore the honor due His name. The incredible thought is that because of His grace, He invites us to join Him in this venture of reclamation.

A second principle is to acknowledge that certain aspects of different worldviews are worthy of discussion.[157] Paul began with the validity of the altar to the Unknown God and then proceeded to lengthen this concept and show how Christianity fills in the blanks. What Paul was saying is, "There is an Unknown God, and I have met Him and know Him and want to share His grace with you." Such discussion leads to the third principle: If there is an open door, then you should eventually share the gospel message, namely, we are separated from God and He has

---

156 Stott, *The Message of Acts*, 279.

157 A book I found helpful for describing the prevalent worldviews is James W. Sire, *The Universe Next Door* 5th ed. (Downers Grove, IL: IVP Academic, 2009). But we must remember that simply knowing the basics about a particular worldview does not mean we understand the worldview.

taken the initiative to bridge the gap and reconcile us to Him; furthermore, we can find fulfillment in Him and live a life that gives us hope now and forevermore. More often than not, the picture we have in Acts 17:15–34 will cover a slowly developing relationship with someone over time rather than a one-and-done meeting, as with Paul. So patience and the leading of the Holy Spirit are part of our arsenal.

The last principle to take from our study is that there is no guarantee that the person(s) will accept our offer of the good news. They may mock or ridicule us, or politely decline our invitation. Such reactions become difficult if we often find ourselves interacting with this person, but we should not give up or write this person off as forever rejecting God. We must not forget, as Luke pointed out, God's Word reached some of the people in Athens; and that is because of the work of the Spirit. Share your words, and the Spirit says, "I'll take it from here."

We often feel pressure in our walk with Christ to be relevant, to be connected to others and considered important to their welfare. But with society being increasingly hostile to our message, we must recognize and avoid the biggest threat to the church. It is not atheism or the political climate; it is compromise, where we seek to be accepted in all circles regardless of what it costs, when "the quest for relevance has degenerated into a lust for popularity."[158] The challenge comes when we accept Jesus' demand that we take

158 Stott, *The Contemporary Christian*, 24.

up His cross and follow Him. Our discipleship is moment-by-moment obedience. And while this mindset will put us in line to hear, "Well done," there is a guarantee that we will suffer persecution in this world (2 Timothy 3:12).

What is being called for is a mentality that reflects the Puritan thought mentioned above—namely that our contribution to community life should be for the common good. We are to be good citizens who fulfill their civic responsibilities. We must pray for our nation, our state, and our community. We should strive to serve others. We can do this by simply offering to pick up someone's mail in the neighborhood while they are on vacation, as well as serving on local boards and supporting organizations that help others who are marginalized or who lack the sufficient necessities of life. Added to these suggestions is the desire to recognize what it means to live in a democracy, with all its opportunities and responsibilities, all its freedoms and limitations, all its challenges to those who name the Name of our Lord Jesus Christ. We must act honestly in all our dealings, following the laws of the land and living out the golden rule as well.

The mood that prevails in our society is pluralism, the position that many differing worldviews are true and that while truth is what you make of it, no particular worldview is more valid than any other. Ideally, this means that all worldviews are welcome to the table as important discussion partners. But, as many are painfully aware, the worldview promoted in this book will not be tolerated in society. We are encouraged to practice our Christian beliefs in private; that is, we are to leave our faith in the attic when we come to the living room of public life, keeping our beliefs to ourselves. What we have is a society that prides itself on pluralism but in reality is intolerant of those who resist pluralism as a valid way of viewing the world. Pluralism, while holding that the private practice of Christianity is acceptable, in effect, promotes a secular mindset, one which seeks to keep God out of everyday life. At best, we live in a society downplaying the importance of God in community life, if not denying His existence altogether.

This attitude is one of the greatest challenges Christians face in society. In his book, *The Case of Civility*, Os Guinness has clearly and logically argued that Christians have certain rights and certain limitations in a democratic America.[159] The first amendment of the Constitution ("Congress shall make no law respecting an establishment of religion or prohibiting the free exercise thereof") does not promote a *sacred public square* where Christianity is favored over other worldviews, including secularism. At the same time, following and expressing one's Christian beliefs are not to be prohibited by creating a *naked public square*, a society devoid of religion. Instead, there should be a *civil public square*, one where all viewpoints are accepted, and all discussion is civil. Evangelical Christianity does not receive such constitutional guarantees, and this places obstacles (or opportu-

---

159 Os Guinness, *The Case for Civility: And Why Our Future Depends On It* (New York, NY: HarperOne, 2008), 77–163.

nities?) before Christians who strive to be *salt and light* in society, especially the workplace. We will tackle vocational issues in our next chapter, but clearly there is much resistance against making our primary call an intentional and visible part of our lives in the community. We are opposed by a belief that insists on "neutrality" and builds its case on "separation of church and state." Both statements strike me as odd, though, since no one is neutral, and the statement about separation is not found in the Constitution.[160]

The holistic demand of the call of God requires that we live as disciples everywhere and with everyone with whom we come into contact. The paradigm from Paul's visit to Athens hopefully provides a broad strategy for personal encounters since we seldom will be in the majority. For the most part, we will find ourselves in the minority, clearly outnumbered by those of a different mindset. Often the majority will make it clear that our worldview is unwelcomed and will not hesitate to downplay, if not exclude, our input. In the name of discipleship, we must have a clear understanding of who we are and what we need to do.

The Bible reminds us that there is a time to speak and a time to be quiet (Ecclesiastes 3:7b). The challenge is to know who we are. If you are an introvert, this is not an excuse to avoid speaking up; if you are naturally an extrovert, it may be a time to hit the pause button and listen. Any such challenge

---

160 The phrase "separation between church & state" is credited to Thomas Jefferson, in a letter addressed to the Danbury Baptist Association in Connecticut, dated January 1, 1802.

can arise in a classroom, a workplace meeting, a community meeting about a proposed business setting up shop in the neighborhood, or a gathering of friends in a coffee shop. In no instance are we not to act as disciples, for the idea that we can pick and choose when to live as Christ wants is not an option.

What really can tie us up in knots is when we support and help an organization with a project that aids those in need, yet at the same time it supports or encourages positions or practices that contradict our lifestyle. While we may not change the direction of the group with whom we are working, we must remember that we are placed in difficult situations for a reason. In some way—through a verbal objection to an idea or our absence at certain events—our witness must come through. Such a strategy becomes more difficult when it is work related, but if we are voluntarily helping in our community, it becomes a little easier to express our disagreement.

One goal during our initial exposure to a group could be to "let your speech always be gracious, seasoned with salt, so that you may know how to answer everyone" (Colossians 4:6). This does not mean that the first thing out of your mouth is the "Romans Road to Salvation"; rather, your speech should be worthy of your Master. A simple reference to how the Lord has blessed you with the talents to contribute to the group you are helping at least puts others on alert to what you are all about. When a situation arises where you must make a stand, may it be that you have already prayed that day to be used by God in whatever situation you find yourself. May your words and actions redeem the situation for God. It does not matter if you are scared; who isn't?! But the Holy Spirit provides the strength to act and the peace to remain calm. And the surprising thing about this is, you will discover that it becomes easier the next time you must stand out as God's person. In fact, you will be amazed to discover that you become more fearful of not speaking up than actually doing so! Even more astonishing, you will be looking for opportunities to witness instead of praying to be spared. Grace is a mysterious adventure.

The idea that genuine discipleship leads to transformation, which is demonstrated through our secondary callings, is based on the belief that obedience leads to revelation. That is, when we act like Christ in the experiences we will have today, we find ourselves understanding better what the Spirit can do in us and through us. The death of Christ is not only our means to salvation but also the model for our sanctification. We have no guarantees that all our work and witness for Christ will be accepted by others or will enhance our standing in our group or community. If we are looking for such an assurance before we seek to obey, then we will be sorely disappointed. But if we obey and discover something new about God and ourselves, then we should take our newfound knowledge and proceed with greater confidence in the Lord and expect His joy to energize us to live for Him (Nehemiah 8:10).

We are not promised applause for our courageous stance or that we will avoid marginalization. The ever-present expectation of political correctness places us in a dilemma. While we do not need to go around looking for ways to irritate people, there may be times that silence portrays a "quiet endorsement" of attitudes we do not hold. This has become painfully evident considering the George Floyd killing, especially with the topics of "Black Lives Matter" and "white privilege" trending in our nation's consciousness. When you find yourself in a group that is composed mainly of your own race or ethnicity, statements will be made that demand some type of response. If you do not respond to statements that promote positions you cannot accept, then silence on your part gives the impression you at least you do not disagree enough to buck the trend, or even more that you accept it wholeheartedly. This thought became critical in the year 2020 with its COVID-19 pandemic and vaccination issues, racial protests, Supreme Court decisions, and an election that devolved into a name-calling and polarizing event. Trying to be civil when attacked is a great challenge and great opportunity for us who want to impact society for Christ. Simply put, we will face the accusation that "if you do not agree with my position or lifestyle, you do not love me, let alone accept me for who I am." Interestingly, you can gently turn that criticism around and ask the person if they feel the same way about you, since they disagree with your way of looking at things.

What we have is a world steeped in tension, being stretched by two opposing forces. We may have the desire and ability to engage in activism in society. We may push for the easing of the racial divide in America, alleviating poverty, standing up for those from abusive homes, the abortion fight, and many other notable and honorable ways of making life better for those around us. You may have found a particular cause to which you dedicate your time and finances. But we must avoid making such activities the focus of our walk with God. They are part of that walk, but they are not the essence of our discipleship. Friction will always exist between my motives and actions. Christ taught us that when we minister to the downtrodden, we minister to Him (Matthew 25:31–46). While we are serving our neighbors, we first of all are serving God. We must make it clear that any good we can offer is from God. This attitude may be rejected and discouraged, but we must discover that we can grow in Christ in such an environment.

We must ask why we are doing what we are doing. Is it to serve Christ and point to Him as our Lord? To help with a need? To draw attention to our generosity? If we are honest, we will probably answer yes to all three questions. Maybe the rarest thing in the world is a pure motive. I must ask myself continually if I have made my service and my standing too important. Have I projected modesty for appearances only, while all the time hiding my pride? C. S. Lewis understands pride as the "Great Sin," to be countered with humility, which "is not thinking less of yourself; it is thinking of yourself less."[161] John the Baptist

161 This quote has also been attributed to pastor Rick Warren in his book, *The Purpose Driven Life: What on Earth am I Here for?* (Grand Rapids, MI: Zondervan, 2002), 148.

said that Jesus "must increase; I must decrease" (John 3:30). Discipleship is a constant series of adjustments to attitudes and opportunities which, no matter how worthy in and of themselves, can lead us to dethrone Christ as Lord. The Greek word "to tempt" (*peirazō*) also means "to test" (see temptations of Jesus, Matthew 4:1–11); and every chance to serve God can also be an occasion to make our service an idol.

While writing this section, I was reading Mark 14:1–11 as part of my daily devotions. This passage contains the anointing of Jesus by a woman using expensive perfume who was subsequently ridiculed by the disciples because they saw her action as wasteful. They complain that the perfume could have been sold and the proceeds given to the poor. Jesus rebukes the Twelve by pointing out that, though they should always be on the lookout for the poor, they were missing the bigger picture here. The poor hold a special place in God's heart (Psalm 9:9–10; 14:4–6; 37:14–15; 69:33), and Jesus is not encouraging the disciples to ignore them. Rather, He is plainly stating that they are showing an amazing lack of awareness at the importance of who He is. The woman has prepared Him for burial, which was to follow His death on the cross. This is the point of the story, for "Jesus in his self-giving love to save humankind is at the heart of the good news. Moreover, the salvation offered to humankind is more than caring about the poor."[162] Service offered in the many ways mentioned above must be kept

---

162 English, *The Message of Mark*, 214.

in proper perspective to insure we remain the dedicated disciples we are called to be.

In similar fashion, we must not reduce our understanding of Christianity to a particular political party. We can easily take up causes that are planks in a party's platform and forget our allegiance to Christ. This was palpable in the presidential election of 2020. Some people equate that a vote for this candidate or that candidate is a vote for or against Christ. The idea of patriotism invites even more tension in the life of a Christian, for how can my allegiance to the USA be balanced with allegiance to Christ? Embedded in our calling to society is the demand to be a good citizen. Yet at the same time, we "must not confuse moral activism or political activism with [our] distinctly Christian spiritual calling to proclaim the gospel to all nations."[163]

We are primarily called to be the salt and light, the examples of holy living for all to see. We cannot be seen if we are not involved in the everyday task of making this world a little better place to live because of who we are and what we do. Nevertheless, we fail to be the light when we are not distinguished from the world. Discovering the grace and demand of God is a lifelong pursuit, and it is learned one obedient act at a time. We simply offer what God has given us, for Jesus praised the woman who anointed Him by saying, "She did what she could" (Mark 14:8a).

May we never forget that wherever we are in the community, there the church is. "In the last analysis, therefore,

---

163 Veith, *God at Work,* 100.

the public success of the church along the front where it faces the world depends upon the measure of sanctification of each individual Christian."[164] May people not see us as being different simply to agitate or lord it over them. Rather, may we live differently to whet their appetite to consider that maybe there is something to Christianity that is permanently transforming and be encouraged to at least consider it. We must never underestimate the importance and impact of dedicated discipleship in our world, our community. "Each of us is placed in a position of great responsibility: the onward march and the resolute stand of the church in the world depends in the final human analysis, on the state of my heart, the quality of my holiness."[165] We are merely sightseers in this world, for our home is elsewhere. But our lives must stand out here if only to resist what we see in our daily walk in the community.

---

164 Motyer, *The Message of Philippians*, 205.

165 Motyer, *The Message of Philippians*, 129.

NINE

Dancing for Joy

A Cambridge student was greatly impressed with a preacher's message and demeanor. He naturally assumed the preacher spent a great amount of time in prayer and preparation for his message, engaged in a vocation that sets him "apart from the din and noise of ordinary life." The young man was more than eager to meet him and jumped at the opportunity to do so when a friend of the preacher offered to arrange a meeting. The meeting took place in a large London counting house where the friend introduced the young student to the man with the beautiful message and calm countenance, sitting at his desk immersed in business. "My young friend is very anxious about your occupation," said the friend. "My occupation, my boy? My occupation is to wait for His Son from Heaven, and meanwhile I make buttons."[166]

I include this story because of the unassuming perspective on the importance of vocation. If anything, our

166 "His Calm and Peaceful Life," Peace Sermon Illustrations, accessed December 15, 2020, <http://www.moreillustrations.com/Illustrations/peace%201.html>.

secondary calling of vocation consumes more time than the others combined. Furthermore, we often look to our vocation for our identity, allowing it to give us purpose and meaning. In doing so, we so easily forget that we have a greater obligation to our Lord. An important component for faithful discipleship is to hold our vocation in a "meanwhile" perspective. In the end, we must honor our Lord in "making buttons" while awaiting His return.

Before proceeding further, I must make some comments on terms we use when speaking about work. A challenge to studying the concept of work or vocation is vocabulary. Many different terms come to mind in addition to vocation, such as profession, occupation, career, and job. Sometimes they are used interchangeably, and other times differentiated by simple nuances. For sake of clarity, I will use profession and occupation as referring to one's life work, usually resulting in making a living as we go along. For reasons that will become clear, I reserve the term vocation for the profession/occupation of Christians. A career is a path people choose that reflects longevity in a profession. A job is a specific described set of duties and responsibilities. For example, I determined that the profession (vocation) God was calling me to was teaching. However, I did fulfill several different jobs during my career. I taught public school mathematics, graduate school theology, and concluded with twenty years teaching of undergraduate students in a private four-year university.

But there is another point that needs clarification. The concept of *vocational calling* is broader than a specific occupation or career; we are called to glorify God in every job or career we find ourselves. In other words, the drive behind our work is our vocational calling, a commitment to bring glory to God whether we type a report, shape a piece of furniture, or write an algebraic equation on the board. This is an attitude we take into the workplace, and we never lose this calling, even if we change jobs or careers. As with our other secondary callings, we are never to forget that we are to be disciples regardless of whether our circumstances change or not.

Work: Blessing or Curse?

When we meet a person for the first time, we often ask (or are asked), "What do you do for a living?" Have we ever thought why this is so? Is it because down deep we believe that we need something besides God to prove our worth? Has our drive or need to be successful in our work become so dominant that we might be surprised to discover that it is more important than our desire to live for God? Why is our "line of work" so often a seduction to idolatry, a path which leads to unhappiness?

The first two chapters of Genesis teach that God created us in His image, and part of our purpose is to work. Adam was commanded to work the Garden of Eden, fulfilling his role as coworker with God. He was God's appointed apprentice to bring a life that flourishes to the world. He would work or cultivate (Genesis 2:15; NASB) the garden, serving God just as we are to do in our work. Simply put, work is "the expenditure of energy (manual or mental or both) in the service of others, which brings fulfillment to the worker, benefit to the community and glory to God."[167]

Work was programmed into our DNA to be a blessing to us. By serving God in our occupation, we can experience the satisfaction of finding our place in the world and discovering that wherever "God calls you to is the place where your deep gladness and the world's deep hunger meet."[168] The words of John Henry Newman (1801–1890) expand this thought:

> God has created me to do Him some definite service. He has committed some work to me which He has not committed to another. I have my mission. I may never know it in this life, but I shall be told it in the next. I am a link in a chain, a bond of connection between persons. He has not created me for naught. I shall do good; I shall do His work. I shall be an angel of peace, a preacher of truth in my own place, while not intending it if I do but keep His commandments.[169]

For some reading this, you have discovered your God-ordained vocational calling and its potential for unlocking

---

167 John Stott, *Issues Facing Christians Today* (Grand Rapids, MI: Zondervan, 2006), 225.

168 Frederick Buechner, *Wishful Thinking* (San Francisco, CA: HarperOne, 1993), 118–119.

169 John Henry Newman Quotes, accessed December 17, 2020, <https://www.goodreads.com/quotes/408029-god-has-created-me-to-do-him-some-definiteservice>.

the possibility of serving others in a meaningful way. Yet this is not the case for all Christians.

Though work was intended to be satisfying for all, it took on the face of a curse after the Fall (Genesis 3). Though cultivating the ground should have provided Adam with fulfillment as he produced fruit to offer to God and his community, it became a source for frustration. Adam flourished while working in the garden as he performed his duties, and this picture reveals that in the beginning work was a pleasure. But all of this came crashing down after Adam sinned. He was expelled from the garden and then told by God:

> Because you listened to your wife and ate fruit
> from the tree about which I commanded you,
> "You must not eat from it," cursed is the ground
> because of you;
>   through painful toil you will eat food from
> it all the days of your life. It will produce thorns
> and thistles for you,
>   and you will eat the plants of the field.
> By the sweat of your brow
>   you will eat your food
> until you return to the ground,
>   since from it you were taken;
> for dust you are
>   and to dust you shall return.
> (Genesis 3:17–19)

We now must work to provide the necessities of life, encountering obstacles, disappointments, futile expenditures of energy, exhaustion, and potential emptiness and feelings of failure. Our vocation is a calling to serve God, but it can easily mutate into drudgery and frustration, sometimes resulting in stress and strife, always being a source that drains our energy and places us in situations that call for choices to put work over family and even God. This perplexes Christians since "a vocation is a task or role that God has providentially called us to carry out on this earth."[170]

The term vocation comes from the Latin *vocare*, "to call," and it is not unusual to take on the mindset of the world and view our vocation or career as the "primary" calling in life. People are normally drawn to specific areas of work by interest and qualifications. Christians and non-Christians alike have occupations and careers. Both have work to do. On a *horizontal level,* then, all people who pursue careers and do their tasks well can make this world a better place; well performed professions are not monopolized by Christians. An atheist can be as devoted to working hard and accomplishing a satisfying career as any Christian can.

Your career may be work performed entirely in one location, working for one company. Or it may entail several different job locations and levels of engagement. For example, one may teach in high schools, community colleges, and universities, eventually serving in administrative positions. All in all, such a career has been about educating others. Even more, we may change careers for numerous

170 Grant Castleberry, "Time and Vocation," *Tabletalk* (Sanford, FL: Ligonier Ministries, September 2020), 18.

reasons and conclude our working life in a different occupation than we first set out to do at a young age.

My emphasis in this chapter is on living out our discipleship in our vocation. We live out our primary calling wherever we work. In other words, our vocational calling is to work in a "timely opportunity for service, in God's providence, presented to believers to enable them to fulfill their vocational calling through what we would call everyday work."[171] My primary calling is to follow Christ wherever He leads me. My vocational calling is to live for Christ wherever I work. My vocation is the means to fulfilling my vocational calling, thus, my vocational calling does not change when I move from one occupation to another; rather, such a calling should demonstrate my discipleship in how I go about working in whatever job I find myself.

When asked to choose which of the secondary callings is the most important, we will be inclined to respond, "It is our home." But the reality is that much of our time and energy will be devoted to the work we do. When acknowledging this, we need to be realistic. Some of us have spent a great deal of money and time on the education or training needed to equip us to pursue and excel in our career. We want our work to be a form of worship in which we "offer ourselves to God." Dorothy Sayers reminds us that "work is not, primarily, a thing one does to live, but the thing one lives to do."[172]

---

171 Whelchel, *How Then Should We Work?*, 79.

172 Dorothy Sayers, *Why Work?: Discovering Real Purpose, Peace, and Fulfillment at Work. A Christian Perspective* (CreateSpace Independent Publishing Platform, 2014), 13.

The quest for a satisfying career is normal for a Christian and should be addressed with all seriousness and dedication. This journey requires a great amount of dedication on the part of one who takes seriously the biblical teaching that work is important. Such is the way of life; it is everyone's hope that their career should be a blessing, but it can easily become a curse in that it unwittingly comes to define who we are. This reality has unexpected consequences for us; our identity is often wrapped up in our career. This situation often leads to disappointment and even depression if it becomes a burden or simply ends, no matter the reason. Simply put, the thinking for today is "no career . . . no identity." We can easily seek our identity in what we do *and not* in who we are, children of God.

Martin Luther taught that all worthy occupations are part of the primary calling.[173] By appreciating our work in light of our *vocational calling* from God, we lift our careers and jobs to a new level. This secondary calling is a commitment that seeks to take the primary calling of God into the workplace and utilize our giftedness, talents, and abilities to meet a need and work with God as co-creators of His new creation. Work that Christians do should bring glory and honor to God:

> For work that is done in faith has a different significance than work that is done in unbelief. The doctrine of vocation helps

173 Roland H. Bainton, *Here I Stand: A Life of Martin Luther* (New York, NY: Meridian, 1995), 181.

> Christians see the ordinary labors of life to be charged with meaning. It also helps put their work into perspective, seeing that their work is not saving them, but that they are resting in the grace of God, who in turn works through their labors to love and serve their neighbors.[174]

Such an understanding provides the Christian with a *vertical component* in their vocational calling, one that energizes them to do all the good one can do to the glory of God: "We are to work, using our talents to glorify God, to serve the common good, and to further His kingdom."[175] To focus on our jobs/careers as a means to bring us prestige and recognition is a temptation we will always fight. And when not careful, we set up our careers as an idol, something that leaves us unfulfilled despite what God has done, is doing, and will do for us. Instead of finding our identity in God, instead of finding worth and security and purpose in Christ, we look to our work to provide this. But if we step back and view our vocations from a broader perspective, we give ourselves the opportunity to see how our work fits into the bigger picture. We are called to serve God by loving and serving our neighbor.

Though many people have professions that can satisfy, I believe that only Christians have the right to call their work a vocation. I mentioned before that for one who is not

---

174 Veith, *God at Work,* 61.

175 Whelchel, "The Biblical Meaning of Success."

a Christian to perceive that their life's work is a calling is to miss a simple yet logical point: You cannot have a calling without a Caller; you may feel attracted to and talented for a particular job and career, but only Christians have been called to their work.

The vertical component of our vocation should separate our work from that of unbelievers, for we believe that our work is intended for good beyond this world. What we do on this earth will transfer into the next world and complete God's new creation in a way we do not understand. It is amazing to consider that when we rest from our labors, our deeds will follow us: "Then I heard a voice from heaven say, 'Write this: Blessed are the dead who die in the Lord from now on.' 'Yes,' says the Spirit, 'they will rest from their labor, for their deeds will follow them'" (Revelation 14:13). The hope that what we do today will be used by God (another example of His grace) to somehow impact how the next world will reflect and worship the living God clearly should separate the Christian from the world, the believer from the nonbeliever—not simply in terms of what is done, but why it is done and if it is done well. Thus, our vocational calling has an eternal perspective for living out our primary calling. That is, "*laborare est orare*, 'work is worship,' provided that we can see how our job contributes, in however small and indirect a way, to the forwarding of God's purpose for mankind. Then whatever we do can be done for the glory of God (1 Corinthians 10:31)."[176]

---

176 John Stott, *Decisive Issues Facing Christians Today: Your Influence Is Vital in Today's Turbulent World* (Grand Rapids, MI: Fleming R. Revell, 1990), 172.

How we conduct ourselves in the present—including how we perform our vocations—is vital to our discipleship. Paul concludes 1 Corinthians 15 with these words: "Always give yourselves fully to the work of the Lord, because you know that your labor in the Lord is not in vain."

> Your work is "not in vain." Why not? Because everything you do in the present, in the power of the Spirit and in union with Christ, everything that flows out of love and hope and grace and goodness somehow will be part of God's eventual Kingdom. That is the message of the resurrection. The resurrection is your new body in which you will be gloriously, truly wonderfully you. The resurrection means everything you've done in the present through your body—works of justice and mercy and love and hope—somehow in ways we don't understand will be part of God's new creation. We are not building the Kingdom of God in that old social gospel sense. We are building for the Kingdom of God.[177]

Put another way, if our efforts "represent the finest works of God's image-bearers, they will adorn the world to come."[178]

---

177 "Let It Flow Out: An Interview with N. T. Wright," *The High Calling* (blog), accessed August 16, 2020, <https://www.theologyofwork.org/the-highcalling/blog/let-it-flow-out-interview-n-t-wright>.

178 Paul Marshall, *Heaven Is Not My Home: Learning to Live in God's Creation* (Nashville, TN: Word Publishing, 1998), 243.

Despite the affirmation of vocational calling, we may never realize the impact a Christian has in the workplace. According to George Barna, only 6 percent of Americans have a biblical worldview.[179] At best, our place of work is constructed to be neutral; at worst we face a "cancel culture." Yet we are called to be God's person at our jobs. We need to recall that the Lord blessed Potiphar's house because of Joseph (Genesis 39:5). This example shows that God blesses one's place of employment through a Christian's work, even if the owner of the business or our coworkers are not Christian. One of the greatest models of working for God in a pagan environment is Daniel. Exiled from his homeland to Babylon and given the name of Belteshazzar,[180] he "resolved not to defile himself" (Daniel 1:8), even to the point of being thrown in the lion's den. He worked in service to King Nebuchadnezzar, skillfully using "his gifts through his vocational calling to transform the culture around him."[181] He was loyal to Nebuchadnezzar, but only to a point; his belief in God would not allow him to become someone other than an open and strong witness for the Lord. He continued to pray to God despite a decree not to (Daniel 6). Daniel "lived in Nebuchadnezzar's house, but [he] belonged to Yahweh."[182]

---

179 Tony Perkins, "The Prophet Elijah and Election 2020: Biblical Worldview Provides Moral Clarity and Political Uncertainty," *Decision* 61, no. 12 (December 2020): 8.

180 A name probably derived from the Babylonian god Marduk.

181 Whelchel, *How Then Should We Work?*, 93.

182 Mark Labberton, *Called: The Crisis and Promise of Following Jesus Today* (Downers Grove, IL: IVP Books, 2014), 107.

Our vocational calling should be one "element of Christian discipleship," a commitment to witness, to influence everyone and every situation for the good of the kingdom of God. This can only be accomplished by the grace of God as He empowers us to live holy lives. We live out our discipleship in our secondary callings in obedience to Christ's declaration that we are the salt and light of the world. No doubt our vocational calling entails our life's work, but we must resist the temptation of the "Promised Land" attitude. Mark Labberton, President of Fuller Theological Seminary, identifies this attitude or syndrome as one that plagues the American church.[183] We in the USA feel entitled to the many blessings our society has to offer; we feel entitled to a flourishing life, and to suffer—especially because of our allegiance to Christ—goes against our understanding of God's will. But, as Labberton points out, we are called to living in exile; we are strangers in a hostile world, and this is never more apparent than in the workplace. The vertical component of vocational calling is not an admission of weakness—just the contrary!

> The *gift of exilic living*, for Israel and now for the North American church, is that it exposes believers to the shoals of authentic faith. When raw reality shoves its way out and demands response, we're given a *gift* that can change our faith. In the Promised

183 Labberton, *Called,* 50–66.

> Land vision, we long to get rid of the dissonance and get the majority of people and circumstances to fit our tastes and values. If we instead admit and understand that we live in *exile*, we realize that the challenges to authentic faith and unexpected love are real and costly. They don't go away in a flash. They are here to stay. They tell us we aren't home. This is the bad news that a good-news people must hear and engage. Otherwise, the good news is not worthy of the name (1 Corinthians 1:2; emphasis added).[184]

If we desire to honor our call to God and follow Christ in discipleship, then we must live for Him everywhere and with everybody. This is an ongoing command to God's people: "You are to be holy to me because I, the LORD, am holy, and I have set you apart from the nations to be my own" (Leviticus 20:26). This Old Testament theme is carried on in the New Testament (1 Peter 2:9). In an amazing example of grace, God views us as "saints" or holy ones because of the work of Christ, for Paul addresses the Corinthians as "those sanctified [made holy] in Christ Jesus and *called* to be his holy people [saints]" (1 Corinthians 1:2; emphasis added). This transformation into who we are in Christ is carried out by the Holy Spirit (1 Peter 1:2). Simply put, Christ's death has made us holy (grace), though

---

184 Labberton, *Called*, 56–57.

we must be constantly exhorted to live holy lives (demand): "But just as he who called you is holy, so be holy in all you do" (1:15). God considers us holy though we are sinful and must continually be urged to "live like who we are." Thus, the Holy Spirit is to live through us for others to see God: "Whoever serves me must follow me; and where I am, my servant also will be. My Father will honor the one who serves me" (John 12.26).

In short, we are called to integrate faith and work, and it appears that the laity have essentially been left on their own to navigate through this minefield. Dorothy Sayers' words of the last century ring true today:

> In nothing has the Church so lost Her hold on reality as in Her failure to understand and respect the secular vocation. She has allowed work and religion to become separate departments and is astonished to find that, as a result, the secular work is turned to purely selfish and destructive ends, and that the greater part of the world's intelligent workers have become irreligious, or at least, uninterested in religion. But is it astonishing? How can anyone remain interested in a religion that seems to have no concern with nine tenths of his life? The church's approach to an intelligent carpenter is usually confined to exhorting him not to be drunk and

> disorderly on Sundays. What the Church should be telling him is this: that the very first demand his religion makes upon him is that he should make good tables.[185]

How do you live a life that is different and yet relevant to the workplace? How do you live out your vocational calling in a world that is not really interested in experiencing God in the workplace, and in a society where most worldviews are free to exist—except biblical Christianity? Is the expression "Contemporary Christian" a contradiction in terms? Are we more authentic in our faith when we fit in with the world or when we stand out as the salt and the light of God? A need is present in the church ("the called-out ones") for its members to receive instruction on how to navigate the richly rewarding yet highly dangerous waters of "living for Jesus in the office." Yet in all of this is the foundational belief of God's grace for us. My prayer seeks to encourage both those who do not think they have a calling because they have never really found a niche in the work world and those who have yet to find traction at work to live a holy life for our Lord. We are "called" to vocational callings and have the opportunity, by God's grace, to live out our primary calling in the shop, in the classroom, and in the checkout lane. Such grace is the context in which we live out our discipleship.

---

185 Dorothy L. Sayers, *Creed or Chaos?* (Manchester, NH: Sophia Institute Press, 1974), 106.

Distorting Our Work

That Christianity has not consistently dealt correctly with the issues surrounding our vocational calling is reflected in church history. For roughly the first 1,500 years, the official position of the Roman Catholic Church was that there was only one true vocation of God and that was the contemplative life (*vita contemplativa*). Such a life was exclusive to priests, monks, and nuns; and this "perfect life" was reserved only for a few, while everyone else's vocation took a secondary place in God's kingdom. Artisans, farmers, and parents followed the "permitted life," the active life (*vita activa*), a second-class life that was simply a matter of necessity.

This two-tiered model is called the "Catholic Distortion."[186] It rejected the significance of non-religious occupations and simply communicated that nothing done outside of the official ranks of the church was important to God. Those in the perfect life had found a "calling"; everyone else just worked. And this distortion is not far from our thought process of today. Even Protestants succumb to the error that only a select few serve God in their occupation. That is, unless your profession finds you in full-time Christian service, you only serve Christ "part-time."[187]

Thankfully, the Reformation championed the position that secular work is as important as work done in the church.

---

186 Guinness, *The Call*, 31–35.

187 Guinness, *The Call*, 32.

Martin Luther led the way, seeing that every Christian has a double vocation, namely the *spiritual vocation* to come to God (2 Thessalonians 2:14; what I designate as the primary calling) and an *external vocation*, the calling to serve others in what we do, especially in an occupation (1 Corinthians 1:1–2; 7:17–20; one of the secondary callings). In short, Luther dropped a bombshell when he wrote this in *The Babylonian Captivity of the Church:*

> The works of monks and priests, however holy and arduous they may be, do not differ one whit in the sight of God from the works of the rustic laborer in the field or the woman going about her household tasks, but all works are measured before God by faith alone . . . Indeed, the menial housework of a manservant or maid-servant is often more acceptable to God than all the fastings and other works of a monk or priest, because the monk or priest lacks faith.[188]

The second-generation Reformer John Calvin (1509–1564) carried on Luther's idea of vocational calling for all believers and, in the process, stressed its importance more so by emphasizing what one's work represents. He thought all Christians have a holy calling to live for God as salt and light in a world that does not recognize that God calls all to come to Him and live for Him. This is the Christian's way of affirming the world as God's creation and gift:

---

188 Edward P. Hahnenberg, *Awakening Vocation: The Theology of Christian Call* (Collegeville, MN: Order of Saint Benedict, 2010), 13–14.

> Underlying this new attitude is the notion of the vocation or "calling." God calls his people, not just to faith, but to express that faith in quite definite areas of life. The idea of a calling or vocation is first and foremost about being called by God, to serve Him within his world. Work was thus seen as an activity by which Christians could deepen their faith, leading it on to new qualities of commitment to God. Activity within the world, motivated, informed, and sanctioned by Christian faith, was the supreme means by which the believer could demonstrate his or her commitment and thankfulness to God. To do anything for God, and to do it well, was the fundamental hallmark of authentic Christian faith. Diligence and dedication in one's everyday life are, Calvin thought, a proper response to God. [189]

Like Luther, Calvin understood that the idea of vocational calling includes a basic attitude of faithfully undertaking an occupation for the glory of God.

It is no stretch to say that the Puritans not only championed the cause of Luther and Calvin in identifying work as honorable and worthy in God's sight, but also refined and clarified it. The Puritans wrote clearly that the call of God is a holistic claim on a believer's life. Following the Reformers,

---

189 Alister McGrath, "Calvin and the Calling of God," June 1999, accessed August 17, 2020, <https://www.firstthings.com/article/1999/06/calvin-and-thechristian-calling>.

the Puritans continued the idea of two callings: the general calling of coming to God for salvation and living a holy life, and the personal or particular calling, where one will find "God's direction into a specific station of life, particularly in the family, marketplace, government and church."[190] The Puritan doctrine of vocation says, "Oh, let every Christian walk with God when he works at his calling, act in his occupation with an eye to God, act as under the eye of God. Serve God in thy calling and do it with cheerfulness, and faithfulness, and a heavenly mind."[191] A key component of the idea of vocation for Puritans was that "the worker be a steward who serves God."

It is widely known that the Puritans encouraged hard work, stewardship, and service. Such reflects the concept of the "Protestant work ethic" of the Reformers and the Puritans. This principle views a life pleasing to God as one which is characterized by hard work and self-discipline (such as initiative and savings) and is a means to serving God and an indication one is saved. Such an outlook may result in material prosperity. Work was a sign of God's grace, though one must recognize the dangers of prosperity as the Puritan church leader Richard Baxter wrote:

---

190 Sam Webb, "Under the Eye of God: The Puritan Doctrine of Vocation for Today (Part 1)," accessed August 17, 2020, <https://erlc.com/resource-library/articles/under-the-eye-of-god -the-puritan-doctrine-of-vocation-fortoday-part-1>.

191 Sam Webb, "Under the Eye of God: The Puritan Doctrine of Vocation for Today (Part 2)," accessed August 17, 2020, <https://erlc.com/resource-library/articles/under-the-eye-of-god -the-puritan-doctrine-of-vocation-fortoday-part-2>.

> Choose that employment or calling in which you may be most serviceable to God. Choose not that in which you may be most rich or honorable in the world; but that in which you may do most good, and best escape sinning.[192]

The goal of the Puritans was "to build a city for God" that they may live for Him and prosper in Him. But when prosperity became a reality, later generations of Puritans lost the zeal and passion for the Christ of the original Puritans. This development in part led the Puritan minister Cotton Mather to comment that "religion brought forth Prosperity, and the daughter destroyed the mother."[193] This laid the foundation for terms such as *work* and *occupation* becoming interchangeable with terms such as *calling* and *the call to follow Christ in discipleship*. In other words, what we have is the beginning of the "Protestant distortion," the replacing of the importance of the primary calling with the idolization of work and occupation.[194] That is, this distortion sacrificed the sacred for the secular and presented a skewed picture of vocational calling. The idea of the primary calling mutated into the call to a profession. Even today a person will share their testimony of how God called

---

192 Webb, "Under the Eye of God," Part 2.

193 Cotton Mather, *Magnalia Christi Americana, The Ecclesiastical History of New England* (Hartford: Silas Andrus, 1702): 59.

194 Guinness, *The Call*, 38–42.

them to salvation and in the same breath share that He was calling them to follow their parents in taking over a business.

Our Vocation

I struggled with the two distortions. For much of my career, I would remark (probably intentionally) that I was "just" a teacher. I was upholding the idea of a two-tiered or dualistic concept of calling, not to the extent that God was not using me as a teacher, but more or less conceding that any participation at my church pleased God more than my work at school. As I became established in my occupation, I felt more comfortable with my vocational calling and less prone to apologize for seeing my teaching in a nonchurch context as of equal importance to those serving full-time in a Christian ministry setting. Part of this battle was lack of direction from the churches I attended, often made more confusing by imprecise terminology. Terms such as *calling, call,* and *discipleship* were not made clear.

While I seemed able to free myself from the trap of the Catholic Distortion, it was not so with the Protestant Distortion. As I look back, I just assumed my call from God was primarily to be an educator. It was not until retirement was on the horizon that I began to reexamine the issue. That is, if my call from God was primarily to be a teacher, would I lose that call since I would retire someday and no longer teach? I had been introduced to the ideas of primary and secondary callings by Os Guinness's book *The Call.* I included this book for reading material in a course specifically designed for students contemplating what their vocation would be. My goal, which I had not processed myself ("do as I say and not as I do"), was for them to contemplate God's call on their life holistically and how it could influence them in the future. Clarity started to come when I read Hugh Whelchel's book *How Then Should We Work?* His discussion of specific secondary callings opened my eyes regarding how to perceive the primary call in all the areas of my life.

Upon retirement I delved into the biblical idea of the call and was surprised to discover how little there is in the Scriptures relating one's call to a specific vocation. What completed the investigation for me was an in-depth study of the Parable of the Talents (see chapter two). Letting go of the common idea of talent as simply skills (often limited to a special few) and taking the broader concept that it refers to all the responsibilities and opportunities God gives us, I addressed the idea of discipleship and vocation, for much of our waking time is devoted to making a living, whether we like our job or not. I simply composed some thoughts on what I had discovered—albeit somewhat late—and eventually ended up writing this book! The truth that our primary call is what initiates our walk with God motivated me to complete this manuscript.

Much of what we discussed in the preceding chapter applies to our conduct in the workplace. We must be ready to be the salt and the light, to avoid the "approval by silence," to clearly show that we can accept all persons regardless of color, belief, or lifestyle. The main difference between our callings to community and to vocation is that we can much more easily walk away from difficult situations in the former than the latter. In other words, we cannot simply throw up our hands in frustration and leave our careers and jobs as easily as compared to those projects we volunteer for on our own time.

This is a difficult topic since we can easily find ourselves stuck in our jobs. "Job lock" is alive and well; when our wage is sufficient, and we have benefits (especially health insurance), we are not quick to give our two weeks' notice. Many questions face us. Are we being asked to do something dishonest or is it that we simply do not like the way our supervisor treats us? Do we have coworkers who ridicule us for our faith or are they doing something that threatens our welfare and success in the business for which we work? What are we to do if we feel we were passed over for a promotion because of our faith or because of lies about us? What about sexual harassment? Vulgar comments? The situation that confronts us is made more intense when we remember the thought of Oswald Chambers that God does not place us where we are the most useful, but rather where we will bring Him the most glory. Even in the proverbial dream job, people or policies or events will qualify as a "thorn in our flesh." The point of Paul writing about his thorn—whatever or whoever that was (2 Corinthians 12:1–10)—was to say that difficult circumstances can be navigated to God's glory:

> But He said to me, "My grace is sufficient for you, for my power is perfected in weakness." Therefore I will boast all the more gladly about my weaknesses, so that Christ's power may rest on me. That is why, for Christ's sake, I delight in weaknesses, in insults, in hardships, in persecutions, in difficulties. For when I am weak, then I am strong. (2 Corinthians 12:9–10)

A toxic work environment makes our vocation painful. Are you pressured for sexual favors for continued employment or promotion? What if a colleague is being pressured? Do you stand up for that person? Are you being bullied to perform illegal or unethical practices? Are you finding yourself caught in the crossfire of racial bigotry of others or yourself? "Turning the other cheek" was never meant to require us to suffer quietly when we are put in demeaning and compromising situations. You may have the option of a human resources department to pursue justice, and you have every right to do so. Turning the other cheek in the workplace comes into play when our causes are upheld and vindicated, and having gained the upper hand, we want retaliation and choose to do otherwise, no matter how much better it would feel to get even.

No magic formula exists to help us decide whether to stay or leave, to keep our paycheck or to give it up. I have the uneasy feeling that God expects us to do what brings Him the most glory. This is the essence of discipleship. If we obey God, we may lose our jobs or at least voluntarily see fit to move on, expecting God to honor our decisions and take care of us. But a replacement job may be a long time in coming, of lesser pay, and prone to more of the same stress. On the one hand, giving up secure jobs has opened doors for new and adventurous vocations for Christ's people; on the other hand, leaving steady employment has led to more difficult times, leading one to wonder where God is in all of this.

Financial repercussions loom large in our decisions about jobs. And while we well know that the love of money is the root of all evil (1 Timothy 6:10), we still have mortgages to pay, cars to purchase and keep up, and others bills that seem to never stop coming due. I would have liked to pick the apostle Matthew's brain for his thoughts after he left his lucrative tax collector position. Perhaps he was trusting God to do for him what He eventually did for the apostle Paul, granting him a simpler life and thus helping him navigate his vocational calling. Paul learned the secret of contentment:

> I am not saying this because I am in need, for I have learned to be content whatever the circumstances. I know what it is to be in need, and I know what it is to have plenty.

> I have learned the secret of being content in any and every situation, whether well fed or hungry, whether living in plenty or in want. I can do all this through him who gives me strength. (Philippians 4:11–13)

He wrote these words from a Roman prison some thirty years after his conversion. He was thanking the Philippians for their gifts to him (4:14, 18), though he wants to be clear that his survival is because of God.

Paul's thought that he "learned (*manthanō*) to be content" carries with it the emphasis upon completion of a task. The term "secret" highlights that what he eventually learned is unknown to many. He has learned to be content (*autarkēs*), to be God-sufficient at all times, for what he means is this:

> I have made my way up through the degrees of progressive detachment from the things of the world, its comforts and its discomforts alike, and finally I have reached maturity on this point. I know the secret; circumstances can never again touch me. This contentment is the mark of a mature believer, and an objective to be cultivated by all believers who want to grow in Christ, who had "nowhere to lay his head." (Luke 9:58)[195]

195 Motyer, *The Message of Philippians,* 218.

Through Christ, he will always be victorious no matter the circumstances. Christ strengthens him because he lives in Christ. He possesses a vigorous faith. "It is finally because of Christ that Paul is contented, and it is Christ whom he offers to us as the means and guarantee of our contentment. For Paul, the person who *possesses Christ possesses all*" (emphasis added).[196]

Though wrong on many fronts, the Stoics appear to have it right when they offer that "if you want to make a man happy, add not to his possessions, but take away his desires." Paul captures the same thought when he writes, "Godliness with contentment is great gain" (1 Timothy 6:6). What this says to us is that our vocational plans and strategies should not be ultimately controlled by jobs that pay well. It may very well be that a lesser paying position with better working conditions is a place where we may flourish. These thoughts will not always alleviate our fears of unemployment and the chaos that could result with extended periods of no income (the COVID-19 crisis has clearly shown what could happen). But we may feel less trapped and "sentenced" to bleak and unhealthy jobs if we take a view that we can be content and satisfied by a simpler way of life.

It should be no surprise that Jesus speaks on the issue of wealth and possessions as much as anything else. He reminds us that "no one can serve two masters. Either you will hate the one and love the other, or you will be devoted

196 Motyer, *The Message of Philippians*, 221.

to the one and despise the other. You cannot serve both God and money" (Luke 16:13). He furthers deflates our egos when He points out that we must "be on your guard against all kinds of greed; life does not consist in an abundance of possessions" (12:15); additionally, we must "not store up for yourselves treasures on earth, where moths and vermin destroy, and where thieves break in and steal. But store up for yourselves treasures in heaven, where moths and vermin do not destroy, and where thieves do not break in and steal. *For where your treasure is, there your heart will be also*" (Matthew 6:19–21; emphasis added).

Perhaps His greatest description of our imperfection regarding worldly possessions is found in Matthew 6:25–34:

> Therefore I tell you, do not worry about your life, what you will eat or drink; or about your body, what you will wear. Is not life more than food, and the body more than clothes? Look at the birds of the air; they do not sow or reap or store away in barns, and yet your heavenly Father feeds them. Are you not much more valuable than they? Can any one of you by worrying add a single hour to your life? And why do you worry about clothes? See how the flowers of the field grow. They do not labor or spin. Yet I tell you that not even Solomon in all his splendor was dressed like one of these. If that is how

> God clothes the grass of the field, which is here today and tomorrow is thrown into the fire, will he not much more clothe you—you of little faith? So do not worry, saying, "What shall we eat?" or "What shall we drink?" or "What shall we wear?" For the pagans run after all these things, and your heavenly Father knows that you need them. But seek first his kingdom and his righteousness, and all these things will be given to you as well. Therefore do not worry about tomorrow, for tomorrow will worry about itself. Each day has enough trouble of its own.

The words "but seek first his kingdom and his righteousness" should characterize living out our primary call in our home, church, community, and vocation, for "the person who does not seek the kingdom first does not seek it at all."[197] This failure can expose our search for security in our jobs, thus revealing our lack of a "divine Center" and exposing that our need for security "has led us into an insane attachment to things. We really must understand that the lust for affluence in contemporary society is psychotic."[198] All this is to say that while living out our discipleship, we

197 Richard J. Foster, *Celebration of Discipline: The Path to Spiritual Growth* (New York, NY: Harper SanFrancisco, 1998), 87.

198 Foster, *Celebration*, 80.

can prepare for the times when our income will be less than what we are used to, including retirement.

The preceding words on a simpler lifestyle will not eliminate all our qualms about losing income due to our needing to look elsewhere for employment when our faith places us on a collision course with an intolerable work situation. But hopefully they will lessen the need to revert to worldly thinking and simply "bite the bullet" to get a paycheck. Even the idea of overtime can become an obsession if we think only of a bigger paycheck and don't take into consideration how it limits our time with our families or our activities at church.

I hope my words on the blessings of and challenges to enjoying and living out our discipleship in meaningful and rewarding vocations have provided some food for thought. But before closing this section, I want to note other situations that hold the same place in some of our lives as do the traditional vocational calling. Some of us have the vocation of simply "working to bring home a paycheck." Such people deserve our utmost respect. Either because of financial needs, or the lack of time for securing essential training and experience, or intentionally not pursuing vocational opportunities available to us in order to serve others, we wind up using our skills and opportunities to provide a living for ourselves and a family. This thinking includes a spouse—usually the wife—who postpones or forgoes a career to put her husband through school to achieve his goal. I was undeservedly blessed with a spouse who did just that, and I will be eternally grateful!

Another vocation often overlooked is those who stay at home. This takes a special person to face the daily grind of taking care of a family, sometimes including homeschooling (which was not optional during the COVID-19 crisis). Also, those in retirement have a new "career" consisting of watching a sick grandchild at a moment's notice, as well as being the "go-to person" for church or civic needs. And a vocation that often goes unnoticed is that of caregiving. Such situations require a cutback on time spent in the traditional vocation, even to the point of giving up one's career for the well-being of a loved one. This is in addition to missing out on family or church or community activities. One such caregiver remarked, "Caregiving is the hardest job I have ever had!"

Our work is to be important and sacred, but never more important than God. It is to be a way to worship God and witness to what He has done in our lives even as we live in a secular society. Yet, to be realistic, our witness is probably not going to change the philosophy of our workplace, even though we are called to be faithful all the while. In addition, we are not to let the world mold us into what it thinks, but we are to be transformed by the Holy Spirit and allow the love and truth of God to shine through us. The achievement of a successful career/occupation can be a wonderful way of showing the grace that God has given us. But such success is burdened with temptations and seductions. Our work and career can easily become an idol, which leaves us open to following the way of the world and drifting away from God. This can lead to us living lives of diminished callings elsewhere. The call of God is what is emphasized in Scripture, and this should impact all our secondary callings. The importance and allurement of our vocational calling is the reality in which we live. Our fallen and sinful natures will prevent us from reaching perfection in this lifetime. But we still must strive for it, growing in Christ and maturing to be what He envisioned for us.

In short, our vocation, while potentially a reservoir of great blessing, can be a snare and often a burden and not a blessing. Yet we are called to be the salt God uses to ensure His holiness is present in the workplace and the light to show His glory in the venue in which we work. Though it will be difficult at times, we should bathe our workplace in prayer. Lift the business or organization up to God in hopes that today will be one of peace in the office. We need to pray for our supervisor, coworkers, and customers. Specifically, we should petition God that we may be used of Him to improve the environment where we work; that those around us may find salvation; and that the customers with which we come in contact will be blessed.

For all we do in our vocation, the words of Martin Luther should guide us all. If we clearly understood a "theology of vocation," we would, like a servant girl over 500 years ago:

> Dance for joy and praise and thank God; and with her careful work, for which she receives sustenance and wages, she would obtain a treasure such as those who are

> regarded as the greatest saints do not have. Is it not a tremendous honor to know this and to say, "If you do your daily household chores, that is better than the holiness and austere life of all the monks? Moreover, you have the promise that whatever you do will prosper and fare well. How could you be more blessed or lead a holier life, as far as works are concerned? In God's sight, it is actually faith that makes a person holy; it alone serves God, while our works serve people. Here you have every blessing, protection, and shelter under the Lord, and what is more, a joyful conscience and a gracious God who will reward you a hundredfold.[199]

We are called to work for God wherever He chooses to place us. This is our vocational calling. He gifts us for particular vocations, whether they fit the traditional definition or not. The place where we feel most useful outside the home is to be consecrated to God, for it is holy ground we walk on.

---

199 Timothy J. Wengert, *The Augsburg Confession: Renewing Lutheran Faith and Practice* (Minneapolis, MN: Fortress Press, 2020), 271.

TEN

Don't Despise the Small Things

English physician and author A. T. Schofield (1846–1929) found himself in a train station at 2:00 a.m. on his journey home. It was a cold and bleak winter's night, and the next train would not arrive for at least five hours. The station was extremely drafty and dreary as he settled in the waiting room. The only other person in the station was a porter, whom Schofield found sweeping. But what caught his attention was the "happy, patient look" on the face of the porter. As Schofield tells it:

> "Are you here all night?" I said.
>
> "For many, many years, sir, I've been on night duty here; but I'm almost worn out now."
>
> "It must be very cold for you; you don't look very strong."
>
> "No, sir, I'm not, and I'm almost racked to death with the rheumatics, but oh, sir, I've had such a blessed time this

night, although the cold has gone right through my old bones."

Curious to know, and but half suspecting the old porter's source of comfort, I said that there was not much comfort in being frozen to death with cold.

"Oh, sir," said the old man, his face all lighting up, "it is not that, but what I've been a-thinking of before you came in was that blessed Jesus; and what love it was of Him to go and take a body that could feel, and go through all His sorrow and suffering down here that He might be able to understand all my cold and pain this night, while He's up there in Heaven. I know His feeling for me, and He knows and understands all I suffer; and when I think of Him a-feeling for me and loving me up there, I seem as if I didn't half mind the pain. Oh, 'tis a wonderful thing—His love—isn't it, sir?"

Through God's mercy, I was enabled to share my fellow-pilgrim's enjoyment of the Good Shepherd's love, and a happy time we spent together talking of the One dear to both our hearts.[200]

---

200 "Wonderful Love," Love Sermon Illustrations, accessed January 15, 2021, <http://www.moreillustrations.com/Illustrations/love%204.html>.

The porter teaches us the amazing truth that no matter who or where we are, we can be used of God in a special way. Society would seek to honor Schofield and pass over the porter. Even when both were mentioned as followers of Christ, by default Schofield would be considered the servant with greater value. But God positions His people with different opportunities and resources. Schofield's importance would be broadcast and noted by more people than that of the porter. Yet I would venture the porter was situated to be as much a "divine appointment" as was the doctor, if not more so.

Paul teaches that we are blessed in the present by the God and Father of our Lord Jesus Christ, "who has blessed us in Christ with every spiritual blessing in the heavenly realms" (Ephesians 1:3). If we stop and ponder that statement, we conclude:

> Every blessing of the Holy Spirit has been given us by the Father if we are in the Son. No blessing has been withheld from us. Of course we still have to grow into maturity in Christ, and be transformed into his image, and explore the riches of our inheritance in him. Of course, too, God may grant us many deeper and richer experiences of himself on the way. Nevertheless already, if we are in Christ, every spiritual blessing is ours.[201]

---

201 Stott, *The Message of Ephesians*, 35.

Furthermore, we have been raised with Christ:

> Since, then, you have been raised with Christ, set your hearts on things above, where Christ is, seated at the right hand of God. Set your minds on things above, not on earthly things. For you died, and your life is now hidden with Christ in God. (Colossians 3:1–3)

We live in the presence of Christ who is seated at the right hand of God (Ephesians 2:6). We have access to God and—by grace—He demands (invites) us to live for Him on earth. Thanks be to God for the inexpressible gift of His grace! (2 Corinthians 9:15). The porter strikes me as one who knew what Paul was talking about. So much is ours, but we must not be ignorant of or even negligent about what we possess.

Read the Fine Print

I read recently of a married couple who skimped and saved in order to enjoy what amounted to their first real vacation in many years. In fact, it was to double as a much-delayed honeymoon. Their trip to the Caribbean was picture perfect and especially relaxing for Karen, the wife. But her husband, Bob, was bothered by the money they were spending. Dining out was taking more money than they had budgeted, so shopping and souvenir hunting were eliminated. They avoided the restaurant in the hotel where they were staying because of the expensive menu and lunched daily at a local Subway. Occasionally, they dined at nearby restaurants; and even though these outings were less expensive than eating at the hotel, they cost more than they were accustomed to.

When Bob was checking out for their return home, the hotel associate asked if he would complete a survey on the hotel's restaurant. Bob replied that they had not eaten there, and when the associate checked the computer to finalize the checkout, he reported that the paid visit to the hotel was "all-inclusive," meaning all meals were paid for in advance. Bob's failure to read the fine print describing the amenities to which they were entitled resulted in the couple missing out on a huge benefit.

I note this story because our lack of knowledge of what is available to us in Christ can produce a similar outcome. We can easily overlook the "fine print" of our position in Christ. We note the wonderful love of Jesus that the porter spoke about when he exclaimed, "Oh, 'tis a wonderful thing—His love—isn't it, sir?" This statement echoes a prayer of Paul:

> And I pray that you, being rooted and established in love, may have power, together with all the Lord's holy people, to grasp how wide and long and high and deep is the love of Christ, and to know this love that surpasses knowledge—that you may be filled to the measure of all the fullness of God. (Ephesians 3:17–19)

We must come to the knowledge of what kind of life is available to us, and in the process of discovering and appropriating all of this, we should exhibit obedience, which pleases God and places us in a position to be blessed (1 John 5:15). These blessings are unavailable to non-Christians (1 Corinthians 2:14) and often unclaimed by Christians. Those who follow Christ must obey Him to receive the Holy Spirit's illumination that can enlighten their hearts. We have at our disposal a new life, a new perspective, and a new identity—blessings to be discovered as we grow in Christian maturity. And this maturity comes from our knowledge of God, faith in Him, and obedience to Him.

The maturity Paul speaks of is a process; though we may reach a certain level in our lives, we will never reach full maturity until the next life. Christian maturity is simply Christlikeness:

> We are as mature as we are like Christ, and no more. He was the only fully mature man. His character was complete, well balanced, and perfectly integrated. All His qualities and capacities were perfectly attuned to the will of His Father, and this is the model, the standard God has set for us.[202]

---

202 J. Oswald Sanders, *In Pursuit of Maturity*, (Grand Rapids: Lamplighter Books, Zondervan Publishing House, 1986), 19–20.

Paul's goal for all disciples is to be mature in Christ (Colossians 1:28–29). The wisdom needed for the disciple who wants to genuinely follow Christ is reflected in the one who can say, "I no longer live, but Christ lives in me" (Galatians 2:20b). But such a reality is found only in living for Him and coming to a knowledge that this is the only life worthy of our Lord. Paul's prayer above says, "When my life is focused on taking God's name everywhere I go, I will discover that the resurrection power that raised Christ from the dead is available to me!" In other words, the Holy Spirit will give me the power that allows me to see as Christ does, and to grasp that all I am is from Christ. To fail to claim my "amenities" is to put me in danger of missing out on the blessings that are mine; I am no different than Bob and Karen.

Oswald Chambers reminds us that the "true expression of Christian character is not in good-doing, but in God-likeness. If the Spirit of God has transformed you within, you will exhibit divine characteristics in your life, not just good human characteristics."[203] We must remember that good works and kindness do not make us a Christian, though they will make known that we are a Christian. We will come to the realization that a life of obedience is not simply achieving a life worthy of our Lord but also reaching a level that is befitting those who are called by His name. However, our sinful nature is used by Satan to convince us

---

203 Oswald Chambers, "The Divine Rule of Life," Devotion for September 20, *My Utmost for His Highest* (Bloomington, MN: Garborg's Heart 'n Home, Inc., 1992).

that the life of discipleship presented in this book is either too hard or ultimately unfulfilling. We fail to understand that the way of the cross is both hard, yet easy. Though that sounds counterintuitive, this is exactly what our Lord taught.

We discover this when we take on the yoke of Christ. This thought is found in the well-known invitation of Christ:

> Come to me, all you who are weary and burdened, and I will give you rest. Take my yoke upon you and learn from me, for I am gentle and humble in heart, and you will find rest for your souls. For my yoke is easy and my burden is light. (Matthew 11:28–30)

The thought behind taking on Jesus' yoke is "entering into submission to" Him.[204] But His ending words of the passage can be confusing. How can His yoke be easy and His burden light? After all didn't He say, "Whoever wants to be my disciple must deny themselves and take up their cross and follow me" (16:24)? Can this be easy? Actually yes, for the word translated *easy* (*chrēstos*) means "well-fitting." When oxen were fitted with yokes in Jesus' day, they were taken to a carpenter who took measurements, then roughed out a yoke, to be followed up by further fittings until it fit

204 William Barclay, *The Gospel of Matthew Vol. 2. The Daily Bible Study Series* (Philadelphia: The Westminster Press, 1978), 17.

well on the ox and did not rub or irritate the neck. "The yoke was tailor-made to fit the ox."[205] What Jesus is saying to us is "my yoke fits you well." This means "the life I give you is not a burden to gall [irritate] you; your task is made to measure to fit you."[206] Wherever your life of discipleship takes you, God's grace equips you with what you need to be a faithful disciple. Furthermore, our burden is "light," not meaning it is easy to carry. Rather:

> It is laid on us in love; it is meant to be carried in love; and love makes even the heaviest burden light. When we remember the love of God, when we know that our burden is to love God and to love men, then the burden becomes a song.[207]

This was the song that the porter was singing when Dr. Schofield found his way to the train station.

The freedom the Spirit offers is the only path to true fulfillment and true service to God. The one who accepts Christ as Savior will not be forced to live a life that pleases Him. But those who voluntarily take up the cross and His yoke will find life in abundance (John 10:10). We are called to learn from Christ and to accept His demands, for to do so will lead to rest and release from a purposeless life. The easy and light designations are indicators:

---

205 Barclay, *The Gospel of Matthew*, 17. Legend has it that Jesus made the best ox-yokes in the region.

206 Barclay, *The Gospel of Matthew*, 18.

207 Barclay, *The Gospel of Matthew*, 18.

> We have an intimate relationship with the One who calls, "Come to me" and "learn from me." As complicated as life may become, discipleship is at heart simply walking with Jesus in the real world and having him teach us moment by moment how to live life his way.[208]

C. S. Lewis said as much when he pointed out that in the beginning discipleship is a hard thing to do:

> You have to hand over your whole self—all your wishes and precautions—to Christ. But it is far *easier* than what we are all trying to do instead. For what we are trying to do is to remain what we call "ourselves," to keep personal happiness as our great aim in life, and yet at the same time be "good" (emphasis added).[209]

We simply want a Savior but not a Lord: "We want someone to save our souls, but not rule our world."[210]

But we must remember that "Jesus can be our Saviour only because he is Lord."[211] The grace and demand of God are beautifully blended in this thought. We recall that the indicative of grace, what God has done for us, partners with

---

208 Wilkins, *Matthew*, 425.

209 Lewis, *Mere Christianity*, 197–198.

210 Wright, *Simply Jesus*, 5.

211 R. C. Lucas, *The Message of Colossians and Philemon: The Bible Speaks Today* (Downers Grove, IL: InterVarsity Press, 1980), 89.

the imperative, what God wants us to do in Him. When we marry, we make promises, which when offered during the wedding ceremony, must be understood as demands, or else the marriage relationship will be doomed. Yet the "have to's" eventually become the "want to's" as our love for our spouse grows in commitment and flourishes. Grace and demand merge into a life that sees God's grace working continually as one acts on His demand to become like Him. "People know what they ought to do; how can they be motivated to do it? Here is an aspect of the doctrine of sanctification (that is, of the process of becoming like Christ) which is much emphasized in the Bible and much neglected in the contemporary church."[212]

When our life simply becomes our means to glorify God and not to promote ourselves or to fulfill some legalistic checklist, He will reward us with a deeper fellowship with Him and with other believers. We should not miss that there is something "in it for me." The idea of reward for obedience is found in the Scriptures. As early as Genesis 15:1 (ESV), we see that "the word of the LORD came to Abram in a vision: 'Fear not, Abram, I am your shield; your reward shall be very great.'" No doubt our greatest reward is being known by God and enjoying Him eternally (John 17:3), for we shall see His face (Revelation 22:4). The concept of rewards can be a legitimate motive for obedience, though we must keep in mind that we do not deserve any rewards for doing what is demanded of us. Such blessings are another example of

---

212 Stott, *The Message of Ephesians*, 195–196.

God's grace but part of receiving the gifts He gives us and making these personalized treasures our own is learning that the life of faithful discipleship is simply a better way to live. A reward will be given to the persecuted (Matthew 5:12) as well as those who give up the riches of this world for God's way, as did Moses (Hebrews 11:26). We come to learn that life is simply better if we obey God. So much better, in fact, that we come to understand that our loving God and neighbor is good for us (Colossians 3:24). The demands of grace open up God's storehouse from which we are rewarded in this life with at least a sample of what awaits the "good and faithful disciple."[213] But, reader, beware: The rewards are primarily of the spiritual variety, not those that position us to live a materially prosperous and healthy life.

While dealing with the rich young ruler, Jesus astonished His disciples by announcing that "it is easier for a camel to pass through the eye of a needle than for a rich man to enter the kingdom of God" (Matthew 19:24). Peter remarks that the twelve apostles have left everything for Jesus and then asks, "What's in it for us [for me!]?" (19:27). Jesus answers that there is much that will be given to the disciples in this life, as well as the life to come (Luke 18:30). Those who leave the comforts of material security and family intimacy "for [Jesus'] sake and the gospel" (Mark 10:29) will "find a new family in the community of faith."[214] But

---

213 Rewards include the idea of crowns: see 2 Timothy 4:8; 1 Peter 5:4; James 1:12; Revelation 2:10.

214 H. Preisker, *misthos*, in Bromiley *Theological Dictionary*, 602.

our reward in this life for faithful obedience comes in light of our taking up our cross and following Him. We will have persecutions (10:30), and our reward will have more to do with serving God and less to do with what pleases or satisfies our worldly nature. Fundamentally, our hope "is other-worldly."[215] Peter left his family and fishing business and Matthew a lucrative tax office; but there is no record that such obedience resulted in either one winning the lottery! But something better awaited them; the ultimate reward was Christ Himself!

God demands obedience for our sake, yet Jesus' discussion with Peter about rewards for obedience "incentivizes discipleship."[216] God demands obedience, "but the reward far exceeds what is deserved, and it is thus a matter of divine generosity [grace] rather than human merit."[217] If we want to allow our primary calling to inform and energize our secondary callings, then we must acknowledge *and* appropriate our spiritual blessings available to us to reach our potential as disciples. As Dr. Tony Evans says:

> [Jesus] says the thing you left, you left the house, he says he will receive a hundred times houses. You left relationships, you

---

215 Alan Cole, *The Gospel According to St. Mark: Tyndale New Testament Commentaries* (Grand Rapids: Eerdmans, 1979), 166.

216 Tony Evans, "The Reward of Discipleship," *Sermons.love*, accessed January 18, 2021, <https://sermons.love/tony-evans/3089-tony-evans-the-rewards-of-discipleship.html>.

217 H. Preisker, *misthos*, 603.

> will receive a hundred times relationships. You left the farm, you will receive a hundred times farms. He says the thing you gave up, you actually never lost, but you felt like you lost it when you lost it, 'cause you lost it and you feel the loss, but God says that's not the end of the story. What you think you lose by becoming a disciple, you actually don't lose, 'cause he says you will receive—that is multiplied: houses, relationships, businesses, lands.[218]

The words "well done" are an invitation to enter and nurture a loving walk with Christ, which leads to a reward, not in that we earn something extra, but in that we discover what has been ours all along. What may lead us to miss the reward of this proclamation is that we can so easily forgo the opportunity to see every second of every day is to be lived as a disciple of Christ. We must be prepared to live out our primary calling, acknowledging that our God has sovereignly set us apart for Him in each of our secondary callings. Yet unless we take to heart His offer of intimacy, fellowship, and identity, and seek to embrace and flourish in these areas, we demonstrate that faithful discipleship is not important. We reflect the mindset that we are a believer but not a follower. For us to thrive in our secondary callings, we must accept and carry out the prerequisites that are part

---

218 Tony Evans, "The Reward of Discipleship."

and parcel of the grace/demand of discipleship: growing in intimacy with God, desiring Him more and more, and finding all we need is in Him. As Stanley Hauerwas liked to say, "Discipleship is like bricklaying—both are difficult but learnable crafts that require skill, language, commitment, and mentorship."[219] We must prove that we understand the fine print, one word at a time.

The Great Discovery

The porter's attitude should be the model for all disciples of Christ. He had made *the great discovery*, namely that the demands of grace are really invitations to show our love for Christ and become like Him (1 John 5:3). This breakthrough is made when we comprehend the rewards of embracing the gospel. The gospel is not only for the lost; it is also for the found:

> For this reason, since the day we heard about you, we have not stopped praying for you. We continually ask God to fill you with the knowledge of his will through all the wisdom and understanding that the Spirit gives, so that you may live a life worthy of the Lord and please him in every way: bearing fruit in every

219 Stanley Hauerwas, "My Top 10 Lessons About Preaching: #10—Preaching Is a Craft," quoted in Matt Woodley's *Preaching Today* Newsletter, March 29, 2021.

> good work, growing in the knowledge of God. (Colossians 1:9–10)

But head knowledge does not imply comprehension of who God is. Yes, we need to study and know doctrinal and biblical truths. But unless we put into practice what is available to us, we have failed to grow in the knowledge of God and His ways.

In my former life, I earned my undergraduate degree in mathematics. Occasionally I would teach a course on college algebra. One of the critical skills was solving linear equations. Often I would list the steps to follow in order to determine the correct solution. Students would memorize these steps and, when guided in class, would usually arrive at the correct answer. Yet when they returned the following day, I discovered they had been unable to solve similar equations as homework. My only conclusion was they had not mastered the skill. In other words, the knowledge of what should be done amounted to little if their skill set did not produce the desired result.

Likewise, we can know the "steps to solving" the equation of discipleship, for we "have it all" from the moment we accept Christ.[220] The challenge is that though we may know how to live, such knowledge remains useless until we put it into practice. We have all we need in Christ—as the porter demonstrated; it is for us to show we can use this knowledge to live a life pleasing to God, one that will

---

220 Lucas, *The Message of Colossians and Philemon*, 36.

continue to grow in the knowledge of Him. Unless we obey, we really do not know how to live; lack of obedience means we are not living as the salt of the earth or the light of the world.

What I hope my readers have learned is that the gospel is a wonderful union of grace and demand. These two aspects work simultaneously to produce the disciple we can become. Grace works itself out in our lives only if we acknowledge that we must work out our salvation in everyday living. As Paul reminds us, we need God's help to even commit to His way of life, let alone to have the power to live a life worthy of our Lord (Philippians 2:12–13). Potentially, the demand of grace will become—if we allow it—a greater and greater desire to do all we can to become the person He wants of us. To hear the blessed words "well done" should be more than a goal; it should be a description of who we are. Obedience ceases to be something we check off our to-do list and instead becomes such a natural part of our lives (our second nature) that we do not realize there is any other way to live, "for to live our life in the conscious presence of our Father is both an immeasurable privilege and a constant challenge to please him."[221]

Since most of our discipleship will be lived in the everyday routines, we must make sure that we desire—even crave—to take the Lord's name everywhere we go. But reality dictates that we live in a fallen world, and it will be a constant battle to live for Him in the ordinary and

221 Stott, *The Message of Ephesians*, 41.

mundane tasks of life. Thankfully, God has set in motion the plan that we be united with Christ and enjoy our riches in Him, no matter our lot in life. Only those who do will position themselves to be described as disciples who live a life worthy to be commended.

What I have presented in this book is the truth that every follower of Christ is eligible to hear their Lord receive them at death (or His return) with the blessed words, "Well done, good and faithful servant! You have been faithful with a few things; I will put you in charge of many things. Come and share your master's happiness!" (Matthew 25:21). We examined this thought in chapter two; our particular level of "talent" is not measured in skill sets, but in opportunities and responsibilities. Some are better suited for the limelight (such as Dr. Schofield) than others because the latter have the personalities to work in obscurity, such as the porter. Every disciple receives abundant grace from God at salvation (chapter three), a grace that must be worked out in their walk with Christ (chapters four and five). Our primary calling is to follow Christ in discipleship and is lived out in our secondary callings of home, church, community, and vocation (chapters six through nine). To ignore this model is to stunt one's joy in Christ, or to discover that Christ never knew you.

"I want to be more like Christ" are words that can easily become no more than a mantra for another self-help program if we do not take advantage of what we are privileged to have. We have sufficient resources to grow in our knowledge of Christ and of what He can do in us and through us. It is one thing to consider God's grace and demands as optional directives for a life of a Christian. It is a tragedy, though, to be ignorant that you already have in you the possibility to embrace them.

We must all answer the question of what gives us the feeling of importance. To have our identity in Christ means we have come to see ourselves as *significant to* the One who calls us; as *servants of* the One who calls us; and as *secure in* the One who calls us. The aim of God is that we find our identity in His Son and not what the world offers. But we will seek this ideal in an imperfect and sinful nature. We must always keep the concept of identity in Christ as the foundation upon which we have built our lives and use it to determine who we are; for even though we will not reach perfection in this world, we strive to grow and attain maturity (Ephesians 4:12–13).

In closing, discipleship is not the glorious path of high visibility, natural success, and constant affirmation of how important we are. Rather:

> Our significance is underlined by Jesus' command to those who would follow to take up their cross too (Mark 8:34–38). This is the true path of discipleship, not the permanently clear, bright and shining way, but the lowly path of service, or rejection, or persecution, discovering daily the joy that is found not necessarily in happy

> circumstances but in faithful service and daily rising with him . . . Faith is to be a daily exercise of walking to where the Lord has gone, believing him to be there and finding him to be so. It is not a procession of cast-iron certainties, but an experience of trust in him who lived, and died, and rose to be with [us] forever. And [we] will find him at home. This is faith and the discipleship to which the gospel has drawn us from the outset."[222]

It is told of a traveling salesman who reported to his supervisor upon returning from his travels that he only had a few orders to submit. After receiving the orders, the manager looked at the man and said:

> "And is this all you've done?" In reply, the man looked steadily at his employer and said, "No, sir, it isn't all I've done, but I'm afraid it is all I can show." In our work for God, it is often when we toil hardest that we can show the least tangible result. But if there has been the earnest endeavor to serve Christ, we may be sure that He knows all about it and will reward us accordingly.[223]

---

222 English, *The Message of Mark*, 241–242.

223 "When We Hadn't Much to Show," Reward Sermon Illustrations, accessed January 15, 2021, <http://www.moreillustrations.com/Illustrations/rewards%202.html>.

I opened this book with the account of Captain Sullenberger III, hinting that he was a great pilot before the miraculous landing. The successful emergency landing had everything to do with his dedication and value to the airline. His greatness is to be measured in his day-by-day routine and only incidentally when fame came his way. His commitment and effort prepared him to react correctly both in normal times and in difficult times. Most of us will never be associated with a "miracle on the Hudson." Rather, continuous devotion is what we need to become the disciples we are called to be, to perform our Lord's work naturally, even automatically, despite our sinful nature. How can we claim to know and love God if we fail to live for Him in everything we do?

Thus, a disciple that will hear the coveted words of Jesus Christ is one who is faithful in the responsibilities and opportunities given by the Sovereign Lord. The follower of Christ depicted in this book will be bold, persevering, double listening, salty and visible, holding to the biblical worldview, a pillar at home and a worker at church, a rock in the community and hard worker in the office. This one will not despise the small things (Zechariah 4:10) but will instead cooperate with the Holy Spirit and allow Him to create the second nature, a holy lifestyle, so as to become the disciple worthy of our Lord. And it is those who have done their best with what they have been given who will see the same hand welcoming them that they took hold of when grace was extended to them here on earth at their conversion. Such a homecoming will be enriched with the blessed words, "Well done, good and faithful disciple, for you allowed My grace to transform you into My dutiful servant, one who loves Me by keeping My commands. Welcome to your home."

For Further Reading

Bonhoeffer, Dietrich. *The Cost of Discipleship* (New York: Touchstone, 1995).

Bridges, Jerry. *Transforming Grace: Living Confidently in God's Unfailing Love* (Colorado Springs, CO: Navpress, 1991).

Guinness, Os. *The Call: Finding and Fulfilling the Central Purpose of Your Life* (Nashville: W Publishing Group, 2003).

Labberton, Mark. *Called: The Crisis and Promise of Following Jesus Today.* (Downers Grove, IL: IVP Books, 2014).

Lewis, C. S. *Mere Christianity* (New York: HarperSanFrancisco, 2001).

Packer, J. I. *Knowing God* (Downers Grove, IL: InterVarsity Press, 1973).

Sire, James W. *Naming the Elephant: Worldview as a Concept* (Downers Grove, IL: InterVarsity Press, 2004).

Stott, John. *The Contemporary Christian: Applying God's Word to Today's World* (Downers Grove, IL: InterVarsity Press, 1992).

Whelchel, Hugh. *How Then Should We Work? Rediscovering the Biblical Doctrine of Work.* (Bloomington, IN: WestBow Press, 2012).

Wilkins, Michael J. *Following the Master: A Biblical Theology of Discipleship* (Grand Rapids, MI: Zondervan Publishing House, 1992).

Wright, N. T. *After You Believe: Why Christian Character Matters* (New York: HarperOne, 2010).

About the author

Richard E. Menninger

Richard E. Menninger is the retired Andrew B. Martin Professor of Religion at Ottawa University in Ottawa, Kansas. He received his MDiv from Central Baptist Theological Seminary in Kansas City, Kansas, and his PhD from Fuller Theological Seminary in Pasadena, California. He has written *Israel and the Church in the Gospel of Matthew*, as well as numerous curriculum and devotional publications. He lives in Basehor, Kansas, with his wife.

www.ingramcontent.com/pod-product-compliance
Ingram Content Group UK Ltd.
Pitfield, Milton Keynes, MK11 3LW, UK
UKHW021650190726
13853UKWH00001B/171

9 798985 211801